Data Science—Analytics and Applications

Peter Haber • Thomas J. Lampoltshammer •
Manfred Mayr
Editors

Data Science—Analytics and Applications

Proceedings of the 5th International Data
Science Conference—iDSC2023

 Springer

Editors
Peter Haber
Salzburg University of Applied Sciences
Puch bei Hallein, Austria

Thomas J. Lampoltshammer
University for Continuing Education Krems
Krems an der Donau, Niederösterreich, Austria

Manfred Mayr
Campus Urstein
Salzburg University of Applied Sciences
Puch bei Hallein, Salzburg, Austria

ISBN 978-3-031-42170-9   ISBN 978-3-031-42171-6   (eBook)
https://doi.org/10.1007/978-3-031-42171-6

This Springer imprint is published by the registered company Springer Nature Switzerland AG
The registered company address is: Gewerbestrasse 11, 6330 Cham, Switzerland

Paper in this product is recyclable.

Organization

Conference Founders and General Chairs

Peter Haber, Salzburg University of Applied Sciences
Thomas Lampoltshammer, University for Continuing Education Krems
Manfred Mayr, Salzburg University of Applied Sciences

Local Conference Chairs

Valerie Albrecht, University for Continuing Education Krems
Stephanie Amon, University for Continuing Education Krems
Thomas Lampoltshammer, University for Continuing Education Krems

Organizing Committee

Valerie Albrecht, University for Continuing Education Krems
Anita Graser, AIT—Austrian Institute of Technology GmbH
Peter Haber, Salzburg University of Applied Sciences
Ross King, AIT—Austrian Institute of Technology GmbH
Jasmin Lampert, AIT—Austrian Institute of Technology GmbH
Thomas Lampoltshammer, University for Continuing Education Krems
Helmut Leopold, AIT—Austrian Institute of Technology GmbH
Manfred Mayr, Salzburg University of Applied Sciences
Robert Merz, Vorarlberg University of Applied Sciences
Michael Mürling, AIT—Austrian Institute of Technology GmbH
Kathrin Plankensteiner, Vorarlberg University of Applied Sciences
Philipp Rehm, Digital Factory Vorarlberg GmbH
Maximilian Ernst Tschuchnig, Salzburg University of Applied Sciences
Gabriela Viale Pereira, University for Continuing Education Krems

Reviewers

Alexander Adrowitzer, St. Pölten University of Applied Sciences
Valerie Albrecht, University for Continuing Education Krems
Laura Bernadó, AIT—Austrian Institute of Technology GmbH
Gabriele De Luca, University for Continuing Education Krems
Damian Drexel, Digital Factory Vorarlberg GmbH

Gregor Eibl, University for Continuing Education Krems
Cornelia Ferner, Salzburg University of Applied Sciences
Michael Gadermayr, Salzburg University of Applied Sciences
Anita Graser, AIT—Austrian Institute of Technology GmbH
Peter Haber, Salzburg University of Applied Sciences
Sebastian Hegenbart, Vorarlberg University of Applied Sciences
Ralph Hoch, Vorarlberg University of Applied Sciences
Ross King, AIT—Austrian Institute of Technology GmbH
Jasmin Lampert, AIT—Austrian Institute of Technology GmbH
Thomas Lampoltshammer, University for Continuing Education Krems
Ivan Majic, Graz University of Technology
Robert Merz, Vorarlberg University of Applied Sciences
Victor Mireles, Semantic Web Company GmbH
Lukas Moosbrugger, Digital Factory Vorarlberg GmbH
Sebastian Neumaier, St. Pölten University of Applied Sciences
Lam Pham, AIT—Austrian Institute of Technology GmbH
Dino Pitoski, University of Rijeka
Kathrin Plankensteiner, Vorarlberg University of Applied Sciences
Dejan Radovanovic, Salzburg University of Applied Sciences
Philipp Rehm, Digital Factory Vorarlberg GmbH
Peter Reiter, Digital Factory Vorarlberg GmbH
Artem Revenko, Semantic Web Company GmbH
Johannes Scholz, Graz University of Technology
Philipp Steurer, Digital Factory Vorarlberg GmbH
Lörinc Thurnay, University for Continuing Education Krems
Maximilian Ernst Tschuchnig, Salzburg University of Applied Sciences
Jessica Voigt, University for Continuing Education Krems
Axel Weißenfeld, AIT—Austrian Institute of Technology GmbH

Preface

Based on the overall digitalization in all spheres of our lives, Data Science and Artificial Intelligence (AI) are nowadays cornerstones for innovation, problem solutions, and business transformation. Data, whether structured or unstructured, numerical, textual, or audiovisual, put in context with other data or analyzed and processed by smart algorithms, are the basis for intelligent concepts and practical solutions. These solutions address many application areas, such as Industry 4.0, Internet of Things (IoT), Smart Cities, smart energy generation and distribution, and environmental management. Innovation dynamics and business opportunities for effective solutions for the essential societal, environmental, or health challenges are enabled and driven by modern data science approaches.

However, Data Science and Artificial Intelligence are forming a new field that needs attention and focused research. Effective data science is only achieved in a broad and diverse discourse—when data science experts cooperate tightly with application domain experts and scientists and exchange views and methods with engineers and business experts. Thus, the 5th International Data Science Conference (iDSC 2023) brought together researchers, scientists, business experts, and practitioners to discuss new approaches, methods, and tools made possible by data science.

The cooperation of the Salzburg University of Applied Sciences, the Vorarlberg University of Applied Sciences, the University for Continuing Education Krems, and the AIT Austrian Institute of Technology demonstrates the strong Austrian scientific footprint and a deep commitment to a cooperative effort for jointly building an international community from science, research, as well as business, through data science and data analytics.

The iDSC is designed as a conference with a dual approach: By bringing together the latest findings in research and science, as well as innovative implementation examples in business and industry, the conference is aimed at reflecting the current scientific breakthroughs and application expertise as a means of stimulating shared professional discourse. The iDSC realizes this approach via its Research and Science track, Application and Use Cases track, and interactive workshops.

Within our research track, a wide range of topics were discussed. These included social media analyses using modern language models, e.g., for detecting hate messages, analyzing vulnerabilities in open-source software libraries, or forecasting models of visitor flows in tourism.

On the practitioners' side, topics such as the challenges of anomaly detection in manufacturing processes or the latest approaches to data ecosystems in the field of supply chains were discussed. In addition, the program was accompanied by four workshops, ranging from "Data Science in Forestry" and "Usage Policies in Data Spaces" to the "Use of Data in the Timber Industry" and the practical workshop "Making AI Accessible for All".

All these activities were complemented with exciting keynotes and panels, providing international exchange and discussing current and next-gen trends in data science. Andreas Böcskör discussed the challenges and potential of a fair data economy, while Sarah Stryeck and Martin Spörk discussed the impact of digitalization and data science on pharmaceutical applications. Besides the named keynote speakers, the panel discussion included Ernst Kössel from the Austrian Ministry of Climate Action, Environment, Energy, Mobility, Innovation, and Technology and Ruben Hetfleisch from Fraunhofer Austria. Here, the participants discussed the future of data science in research and practice, as well as the current research agenda and funding landscape in Austria.

Finally, we thank the organizing and program committee and the reviewers for their help in making the conference a reoccurring success. Enjoy the present proceedings of the conference, and see you in 2025 again in Salzburg!

Salzburg, Austria   Peter Haber
Krems an der Donau, Austria   Thomas J. Lampoltshammer
Salzburg, Austria   Manfred Mayr
                                            Conference Founders and General Chairs

iDSC2023—Organizing Institutions
University for Continuing Education Krems
Salzburg University of Applied Sciences

iDSC Consortium
Salzburg University of Applied Sciences
Vorarlberg University of Applied Sciences
University for Continuing Education Krems
AIT—Austrian Institute of Technology

Contents

Comparison of Clustering Algorithms for Statistical Features of Vibration Data Sets

Philipp Sepin, Jana Kemnitz, Safoura Rezapour Lakani, and Daniel Schall

Abstract Vibration-based condition monitoring systems are receiving increasing attention due to their ability to accurately identify different conditions by capturing dynamic features over a broad frequency range. However, there is little research on clustering approaches in vibration data and the resulting solutions are often optimized for a single data set. In this work, we present an extensive comparison of the clustering algorithms K-means clustering, OPTICS, and Gaussian mixture model clustering (GMM) applied to statistical features extracted from the time and frequency domains of vibration data sets. Furthermore, we investigate the influence of feature combinations, feature selection using principal component analysis (PCA), and the specified number of clusters on the performance of the clustering algorithms. We conducted this comparison in terms of a grid search using three different benchmark data sets. Our work showed that averaging (Mean, Median) and variance-based features (Standard Deviation, Interquartile Range) performed significantly better than shape-based features (Skewness, Kurtosis). In addition, K-means outperformed GMM slightly for these data sets, whereas OPTICS performed significantly worse. We were also able to show that feature combinations as well as PCA feature selection did not result in any significant performance improvements. With an increase in the specified number of clusters, clustering algorithms performed better, although there were some specific algorithmic restrictions.

Keywords Predictive maintenance · Vibration analysis · Clustering

1 Introduction

The constant and accurate monitoring of machinery is a vital aspect of its operation. Vibration-based condition monitoring systems are receiving increasing attention due to their ability to accurately identify different conditions by capturing dynamic features over a broad frequency range [6, 13, 18, 21, 23–25, 27, 28]. Further, low-cost sensors enable large scale operation through various equipment types [10]. In this context, unsupervised learning methods can prove instrumental as a preprocessing step for supervised learning methods or as a stand-alone method when dealing with missing labels. Research in the field mainly focused on classification [1, 6, 9, 11, 13, 16, 18, 21, 23–25, 27, 30, 31] or anomaly detection [3, 10, 28].

What might seem trivial as a supervised classification task bears significant difficulties when done in an unsupervised way. K-means clustering and DBSCAN (density-based spatial clustering of applications with noise) [7] have been explored for condition classification of bearings using vibrational data [17]. While DBSCAN is very sensitive to clustering parameters and has difficulty detecting clusters of different densities, the extension OPTICS (ordering points to identify the clustering structure) [2] was shown to solve these issues when used for condition classification of bearings [12]. Fuzzy C-means clustering (FCM) has been utilized for detecting anomalous conditions of nuclear turbines [3].

Besides the selection of the right clustering algorithms, feature extraction and selection itself is a challenging task in vibrational data since the performance of the clustering algorithm heavily depends on the features. Previous work explored statistical time domain features [5, 20, 25] and frequency domain features extracted by means of the fast Fourier transform

P. Sepin (✉) · J. Kemnitz · S. R. Lakani · D. Schall
Siemens Technology, Vienna, Austria
e-mail: philipp@sepin.at

P. Sepin
Vienna University of Technology, Vienna, Austria

(FFT) [13, 30], discrete wavelet transform (DWT) [5, 10, 13, 30], and continuous wavelet transform (CWT) [1, 5]. The difficulty here lies in the optimal modeling of the feature space to allow for the unsupervised separation of different conditions, which is particularly difficult in the case of industrial data and gets even more difficult with an increasing number of conditions.

Summarizing, there is little research on clustering approaches in vibration data and the resulting solutions are often optimized for a single data set. A fundamental analysis of feature extraction and selection methods, and clustering algorithms validated over several data sets is required. Therefore, we aim to answer the following questions.

Q1. Which combinations of statistical features and clustering algorithms perform best for multiple data sets?
Q2. Does the performance of statistical feature and clustering algorithm combinations generalize for arbitrary data sets?
Q3. Can the combination of several different features improve the performance of the clustering algorithms?
Q4. Can principal component analysis (PCA) improve the performance of the clustering algorithms by selecting the most representative features?
Q5. How does the specified number of clusters affect the performance of the clustering algorithms?

2 Theoretical Foundations

2.1 Clustering

The K-means algorithm is one of the most popular iterative clustering methods. One chooses the desired number of cluster centers and the K-means algorithm iteratively moves the centers to minimize the total within cluster variance [8].

Gaussian mixture model clustering (GMM) can be thought of as a method similar in spirit to K-means. Each cluster is described in terms of a normal distribution, which has a centroid as in K-means [8].

DBSCAN is a density-based clustering algorithm that works by differentiating between low-point-density regions and high-point-density regions. The points are assigned to one of three categories using two density parameters. The different clusters are formed by core and border points [7]. Due to DBSCAN using a global density parameter, it is not possible to reliably detect clusters with significantly different densities. To solve this, several different density parameters would be needed. This is done by the clustering algorithm OPTICS, which works in principle like an extended DBSCAN algorithm for an infinite number of distance parameters, which are smaller than a global distance parameter, which may even be set to infinity [2].

2.2 Statistical Features and Principal Component Analysis

Statistical features can be obtained from the time domain (denoted by *TD*), as well as the frequency domain (denoted by *FD*) by means of fast Fourier transforms (FFT) [14, 22]. In the time domain, these measures are derived from the vibrational amplitudes, in the frequency domain, they are derived from the frequency components. This method can be enhanced by using preprocessing operations like band-pass filters for the extraction of features of specific frequency components. The following statistical features were used.

- Arithmetic mean of absolute values (*Abs Mean*).
- Median of absolute values (*Abs Median*).
- Standard deviation (*Std*).
- Interquartile range (*IQR*).
- Skewness of absolute values (*Abs Skew*).
- Kurtosis of absolute values (*Abs Kurt*).

Principal component analysis is a method for obtaining new uncorrelated variables that are linear combinations of the original variables. Due to the fact, that the principal components are sorted in order of variance in the original data, one has the option to reduce the dimensions of the input vector by only using the first few principal components, whilst still preserving most of the contained information [29].

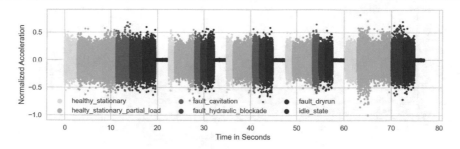

Fig. 1 Time series data of data set 1 with constant components removed

3 Data Sets

3.1 Data Set 1

This data set (Fig. 1) was acquired by SIEMENS for the development of anomaly detection and classification algorithms [11, 16]. A test bench with a centrifugal pump and a multi-sensor [4] was constructed for simulation of anomalous conditions. The three-axis accelerometer of the multi-sensor was used to record 512 samples at a sampling rate of 6644 Hz once every minute. This data set contains the following six conditions.

- Class 0, idle state. The system operates under normal condition.
- Class 1, healthy partial load. The system operates under normal condition with partial load.
- Class 2, healthy. The system operates under normal condition.
- Class 3, hydraulic blockade. The outlet valve behind the pump is closed.
- Class 4, dry run. The inlet valve in front of the pump is closed.
- Class 5, cavitation.

3.2 Data Set 2

This open-source data set (Fig. 2) was part of a publication on the development and evaluation of algorithms for unbalance detection [19]. Unbalances of various sizes were attached to a rotating DC motor shaft. Three single-axis accelerometers were used to record vibrations on the rotating shaft at a sampling rate of 4096 Hz. A statistically representative randomly shuffled subset of this data set was used. This data set contains the following five conditions.

- Class 0, no unbalance.
- Class 1, low unbalance.
- Class 2, medium low unbalance.
- Class 3, medium high unbalance.
- Class 4, high unbalance.

3.3 Data Set 3

The Skoltech Anomaly Benchmark (SKAB) (Fig. 3) is an open-source data set designed for evaluating anomaly detection algorithms [15]. A test bench with a water circulation system was constructed for simulation of anomalous conditions. Data from two single-axis accelerometers was used. These sensors were attached to the pump and recorded vibrations at a sampling rate of 1 Hz. This data set contains the following three conditions. A fourth class that contained several different anomalous conditions was discarded in our case, since such a heavily mixed class is not suitable for unsupervised classification.

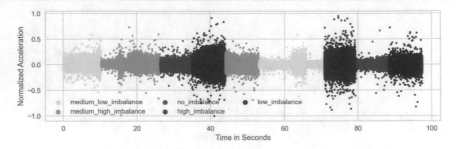

Fig. 2 Time series data of data set 2 with constant components removed

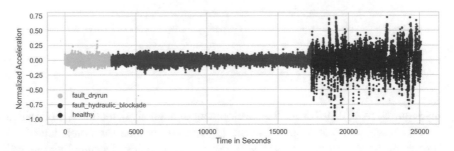

Fig. 3 Time series data of data set 3 with constant components removed

- Class 0, healthy. The system operates under normal condition.
- Class 1, dry run. The inlet valve in front of the pump is closed.
- Class 2, hydraulic blockade. The outlet valve behind the pump is closed.

4   Experiments and Results

The success of the following experiments was measured by the average purity of the resulting clusters. Purity is a measure of the degree to which clusters only contain one single class. For each cluster m, the data points that belong to the class d that makes up the majority of the cluster are counted and divided by the total number N of data points. This metric does not penalize an increasing number of clusters. Therefore, it should always be seen in relation to the specified number of clusters. For each of the following experimental settings, three tests were run.

$$Purity = \frac{1}{N} \sum_{m} \max_{d} |m \cap d| \tag{1}$$

4.1   Experiments

For the following experiments **Q1** to **Q4**, the number of specified clusters was set equal to the number of conditions in the respective data set. For experiment **Q5**, the number of specified clusters was varied. Preprocessing was done by removing the constant components of the data, normalizing it, and applying a Savitzky-Golay filter [26] with a polynomial order of 7 and a window size of 9.

Q1 In order to evaluate the performance of certain combinations of statistical features and clustering algorithms on the three data sets, an extensive grid search was conducted. The four variables of this grid search were the algorithm $\in \{$*K-means, OPTICS, GMM*$\}$, the statistical feature $\in \{$*Abs Mean, Abs Median, Std, IQR, Abs Skew, Abs Kurt*$\}$, and the domain $\in \{$*Time Domain, Frequency Domain*$\}$, which resulted in a number of 324 trials for this evaluation.

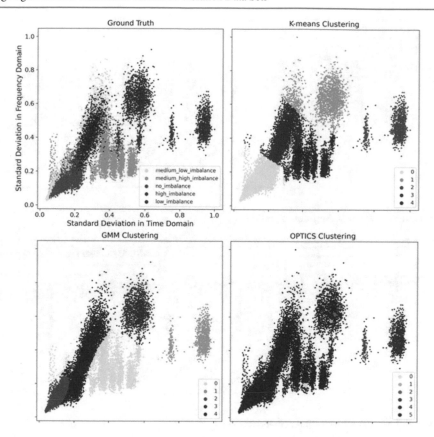

Fig. 4 Feature space of data set 2 with ground truth, and clusters formed by different clustering algorithms

Q2 These results were also used to test the generalization behavior of feature algorithm combinations for the different data sets.

Q3 For the purpose of evaluating the effect of feature combinations on the clustering performance, another grid search was conducted. For each of the algorithms, the three best performing features were chosen. For each of these sets of three features, all permutations of single, double, and triple feature combinations were tested. The three variables of this grid search were the algorithm $\in \{K\text{-means, OPTICS, GMM}\}$ and the feature combinations $\in \{A, B, C, AB, BC, CA, ABC\}$, which resulted in a number of 126 trials for this evaluation.

Q4 In order to test the effect of feature selection using PCA on the clustering performance, another grid search was conducted. For each of the algorithms, the three best performing features were chosen and used as a feature combinations to increase feature dimensionality. The three variables of this grid search were the algorithm $\in \{K\text{-means, OPTICS, GMM}\}$ and the number of principal components $\in \{No\ PCA, 6, 4, 2, 1\}$, which resulted in a number of 90 trials for this evaluation.

Q5 A final grid search was conducted for the purpose of evaluating the effect of the specified number of clusters on the clustering performance and comparing it to the number of clusters proposed by the elbow method. For each of the algorithms, the three best performing features were chosen and used as a feature combinations. The three variables of this grid search were the algorithm $\in \{K\text{-means, OPTICS}\}$ and the specified number of clusters $\in \{Elbow\ Method, n, 1.25n, 1.5n, 1.75n, 2n\}$ with n as the number of conditions in the data set, which resulted in a number of 108 trials for this evaluation (Fig. 4).

4.2 Results

Q1 Fig. 5 shows the average purity per feature for the three different algorithms. In our case, K-means outperformed GMM slightly for these data sets, whereas OPTICS performed significantly worse than the other two algorithms.

Q2 Fig. 6 shows the purity per feature of K-means clustering for the three different data sets. Even though some features seem to be superior for all three data sets, their performance does not generalize for all these data sets. Figure 7 shows the

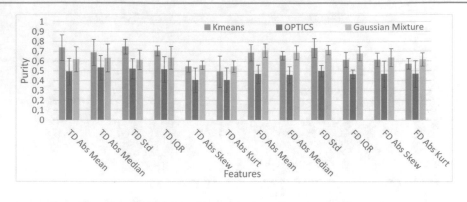

Fig. 5 Average purity per feature for different clustering algorithms

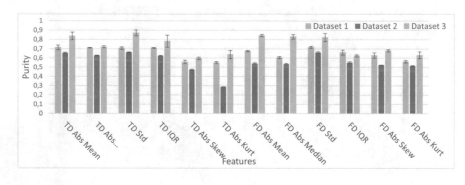

Fig. 6 K-means clustering purity per feature for different data sets

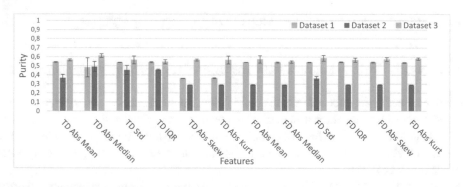

Fig. 7 OPTICS purity per feature for different data sets

purity per feature of OPTICS for the three different data sets. As one can see, OPTICS performed significantly worse than the other two algorithms for any feature. Figure 8 shows the purity per feature of GMM clustering for the three different data sets. For data set 3, GMM performed significantly better using features in the frequency domain than in the time domain. Nevertheless, the performance of the individual features did not generalize for all three data sets.

Q3 Fig. 9 shows the purity for different feature combinations of K-means clustering for the three different data sets. Feature combinations did not significantly increase the clustering performance. The same applies to GMM clustering (data not shown).

Q4 Fig. 9 shows the purity of K-means clustering for different numbers of principal components for the three different data sets. PCA did not have a significant effect on the clustering performance. Except for data set 2, where the clustering performance decreased when using only a single principal component. The same applies to GMM clustering (data not shown).

Q5 Fig. 10 shows the purity of K-means clustering for different specified numbers of clusters for the three different data sets, as well as the purity for the number of clusters evaluated using the elbow method. The clustering performance did not change significantly for $1.25n$, but significantly increased for $1.5n$. A further increase in the specified number of clusters had no effect on the clustering performance. Figure 10 shows the purity of GMM clustering for different specified numbers of

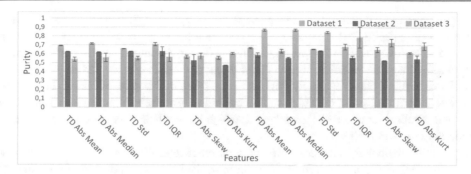

Fig. 8 GMM clustering purity per feature for different data sets

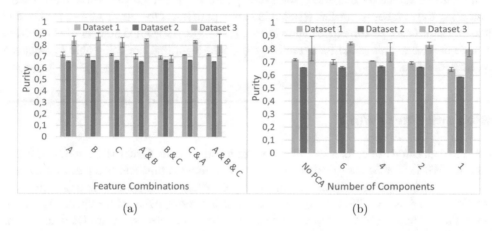

Fig. 9 K-means clustering purity for feature combinations (**a**) and with different numbers of principal components (**b**) for different data sets

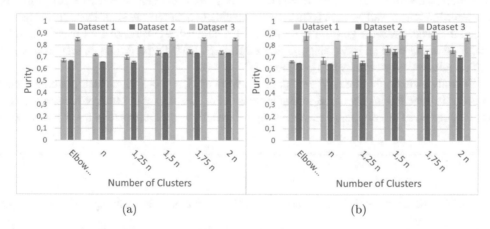

Fig. 10 K-means clustering (**a**) and GMM clustering (**b**) purity for different specified numbers of clusters for different data sets

clusters for the three different data sets, as well as the purity for the number of clusters evaluated using the elbow method. Clustering performance significantly enhanced for an increasing specified number of clusters, until $2n$, where it slightly decreased.

5   Discussion

The high variance in purity shows that there is no general feature that performs best for an arbitrary data set, even though there are some trends for these specific data sets. Averaging (Mean, Median) and variance-based features (Standard Deviation,

Interquartile Range) performed significantly better than shape-based features (Skewness, Kurtosis), even though these are frequently used in the literature [5, 20, 25]. This may also reflect on other shape-based features like the Crest Factor.

Even though OPTICS has proven useful for clustering vibration data in literature [12], it clearly was not suited for the task of clustering these vibration data sets, as can be seen in Fig. 4. Most of the data was labeled as noise by OPTICS. This could be a result of high variance and low class separability in the feature space of this data, which can be seen in Fig. 4. It remains unclear if a more extensive optimization of OPTICS would have led to better results. It can be assumed that OPTICS would have needed specific optimization for every different dataset, which has not been done in this case. Therefore, OPTICS was discarded for the remaining three experiments.

Even though feature combinations for clustering are common practice in literature [5, 20, 25], there was no significant performance improvement. All variations in performance can most likely be traced back to the intrinsic randomness of K-means and GMM. PCA also did not result in any significant performance improvements. It is to note that even a single principal component seems so suffice for clustering, since it only resulted in a slight performance decrease.

As expected, increasing the number of clusters resulted in higher purity. It is to note that for K-means, an increase beyond $1.5n$ did not result in any significant performance improvement. For GMM, a specified number of clusters as high as $2n$ leads to a slight performance decrease. This could be a result of the GMM algorithm not being able to locate any more distinct Gaussian distributions in the data.

6   Conclusion and Future Work

In this work, we presented an extensive comparison of the clustering algorithms K-means clustering, OPTICS, and Gaussian mixture model clustering (GMM) using statistical features extracted from the time and frequency domains of three different vibration data sets. Furthermore, we investigated the influence of feature combinations, feature selection using principal component analysis (PCA), and the specified number of clusters on the performance of the clustering algorithms.

Our results showed that averaging (Mean, Median) and variance-based features (Standard Deviation, Interquartile Range) performed significantly better than shape-based features (Skewness, Kurtosis). In addition, K-means outperformed GMM slightly for these data sets, whereas OPTICS performed significantly worse than the other two algorithms. We were also able to show that feature combination as well as PCA feature selection did not result in any significant performance improvements. The performance of K-means increased significantly for a specified number of clusters of 1.5 times the number of conditions, but did not continue to increase with an increasing number of clusters. GMM's performance increased continuously until 2 times the number of conditions, when it began to decline.

A limitation of our study is that only three different data sets were used, and only three tests per experimental setting were run. This leads to uncertain conclusions about the generalizability of our results for arbitrary vibration data sets. Furthermore, this comparison is also limited to three specific clustering algorithms. Both limitations may be investigated in future studies.

References

1. Altobi, M.A.S., Bevan, G., Wallace, P., Harrison, D., Ramachandran, K.: Fault diagnosis of a centrifugal pump using mlp-gabp and svm with cwt. Eng. Sci. Technol. Int. J. (2019)
2. Ankerst, M., Breunig, M.M., Kriegel, H.P., Sander, J.: Optics: Ordering points to identify the clustering structure. SIGMOD Rec. (1999)
3. Baraldi, P., Di Maio, F., Rigamonti, M., Zio, E., Seraoui, R.: Unsupervised clustering of vibration signals for identifying anomalous conditions in a nuclear turbine. J. Intell. Fuzzy Syst. (2015)
4. Bierweiler, T., Grieb, H., Dosky, S., Hartl, M.: Smart Sensing Environment – Use Cases and System for Plant Specific Monitoring and Optimization (2019)
5. Dhamande, L.S., Chaudhari, M.B.: Compound gear-bearing fault feature extraction using statistical features based on time-frequency method. Measurement (2018)
6. Elangovan, M., Sugumaran, V., Ramachandran, K., Ravikumar, S.: Effect of svm kernel functions on classification of vibration signals of a single point cutting tool. Expert Syst. Appl. (2011)
7. Ester, M., Kriegel, H.P., Sander, J., Xu, X.: A density-based algorithm for discovering clusters in large spatial databases with noise (1996)
8. Hastie, T., Tibshirani, R., Friedman, J.: The Elements of statistical Learning. Springer (2017)
9. Heistracher, C., Jalali, A., Strobl, I., Suendermann, A., Meixner, S., Holly, S., Schall, D., Haslhofer, B., Kemnitz, J.: Transfer learning strategies for anomaly detection in iot vibration data. In: IECON 2021 – 47th Annual Conference of the IEEE Industrial Electronics Society (2021)
10. Heistracher, C., Jalali, A., Suendermann, A., Meixner, S., Schall, D., Haslhofer, B., Kemnitz, J.: Minimal-configuration anomaly detection for iiot sensors. In: Data Science – Analytics and Applications (2022)
11. Holly, S., Hiessl, T., Lakani, S.R., Schall, D., Heitzinger, C., Kemnitz, J.: Evaluation of hyperparameter-optimization approaches in an industrial federated learning system. In: Data Science – Analytics and Applications (2022)

12. Hotait, H., Chiementin, X., Sayed Mouchaweh, M., Rasolofondraibe, l.: Monitoring of ball bearing based on improved real-time optics clustering. J. Signal Process. Syst. (2021)
13. Jafarian, K., Mobin, M., Jafari-Marandi, R., Rabiei, E.: Misfire and valve clearance faults detection in the combustion engines based on a multi-sensor vibration signal monitoring. Measurement (2018)
14. Jenkins, G.M., Watts, D.G.: Spectral Analysis and its Applications. Holden-Day (1968)
15. Katser, I.D., Kozitsin, V.O.: Skoltech anomaly benchmark (skab). https://www.kaggle.com/dsv/1693952 (2020)
16. Kemnitz, J., Bierweiler, T., Grieb, H., von Dosky, S., Schall, D.: Towards robust and transferable iiot sensor based anomaly classification using artificial intelligence. In: Data Science – Analytics and Applications (2022)
17. Kerroumi, S., Chiementin, X., Rasolofondraibe, L.: Dynamic classification method of fault indicators for bearings' monitoring. Mech. Ind. (2013)
18. Kolar, D., Lisjak, D., Pająk, M., Pavković, D.: Fault diagnosis of rotary machines using deep convolutional neural network with wide three axis vibration signal input. Sensors (2020)
19. Mey, O., Neudeck, W., Schneider, A., Enge-Rosenblatt, O.: Machine learning-based unbalance detection of a rotating shaft using vibration data (2020)
20. Obuchowski, J., Zimroz, R., Wyłomańska, A.: Blind equalization using combined skewness-kurtosis criterion for gearbox vibration enhancement. Measurement (2016)
21. Panda, A.K., Rapur, J.S., Tiwari, R.: Prediction of flow blockages and impending cavitation in centrifugal pumps using support vector machine (svm) algorithms based on vibration measurements. Measurement (2018)
22. Rao, K.D., Swamy, M.N.S.: Digital Signal Processing. Springer (2018)
23. Ribeiro Junior, R.F., de Almeida, F.A., Gomes, G.F.: Fault classification in three-phase motors based on vibration signal analysis and artificial neural networks. Neural Comput. Appl. (2020)
24. Romero, A., Soua, S., Gan, T.H., Wang, B.: Condition monitoring of a wind turbine drive train based on its power dependant vibrations. Renew. Energy (2018)
25. Ruiz-Gonzalez, R., Gomez-Gil, J., Gomez-Gil, F., Martínez-Martínez, V.: An svm-based classifier for estimating the state of various rotating components in agro-industrial machinery with a vibration signal acquired from a single point on the machine chassis. Sensors (Basel, Switzerland) (2014)
26. Savitzky, A., Golay, M.J.E.: Smoothing and differentiation of data by simplified least squares procedures. Anal. Chem. (1964)
27. Venkata, S.K., Rao, S.: Fault detection of a flow control valve using vibration analysis and support vector machine. Electronics (2019)
28. Vos, K., Peng, Z., Jenkins, C., Shahriar, M.R., Borghesani, P., Wang, W.: Vibration-based anomaly detection using lstm/svm approaches. Mech. Syst. Signal Process. (2022)
29. Webb, A.R., Copsey, K.D.: Statistical Pattern Recognition. Wiley (2011)
30. Zabihi-Hesari, A., Ansari-Rad, S., Shirazi, F.A., Ayati, M.: Fault detection and diagnosis of a 12-cylinder trainset diesel engine based on vibration signature analysis and neural network. Proc. Inst. Mech. Eng. Part C: J. Mech. Eng. Sci. (2019)
31. Zhao, B., Zhang, X., Zhan, Z., Wu, Q.: A robust construction of normalized cnn for online intelligent condition monitoring of rolling bearings considering variable working conditions and sources. Measurement (2021)

Towards Measuring Vulnerabilities and Exposures in Open-Source Packages

Tobias Dam and Sebastian Neumaier

Abstract Much of the current software depends on open-source components, which in turn have complex dependencies on other open-source libraries. Vulnerabilities in open source therefore have potentially huge impacts. The goal of this work is to get a quantitative overview of the frequency and evolution of existing vulnerabilities in popular software repositories and package managers. To this end, we provide an up-to-date overview of the open source landscape and its most popular package managers, we discuss approaches to map entries of the Common Vulnerabilities and Exposures (CVE) list to open-source libraries and we show the frequency and distribution of existing CVE entries with respect to popular programming languages.

1 Introduction

According to a 2021 open-source security report by Synopsis,[1] 98% of 1.5k reviewed codebases depend on open-source components and libraries. Given the number of dependencies of medium- to large-size software projects, any vulnerability in open-source code has security implications in numerous software products and involves the risk of disclosing vulnerabilities either directly or through dependencies, as famously seen in the 2014 Heartbleed Bug,[2] a vulnerability in OpenSSL which exposed large parts of the existing websites at this time.

Open-source code is written in various programming languages and published in corresponding package managers. Currently, the largest package managers are the platform of the Go programming language and the NPM repository for Node.js, cf. Table 1. The documentation and communication of discovered vulnerabilities, however, does not take place directly at the package managers. The most important platform for discovered vulnerabilities is the Common Vulnerabilities and Exposures (CVE) list [8].[3] It is a dictionary and reference of common and publicly known IT system vulnerabilities, operated by the Mitre Corporation, an American non-profit institution. CVE is a critical source for security management, however, is to some extend an heterogeneous and unstructured source. In particular, it does not include structured pointers and references to package managers (e.g., NPM) and/or the source code in software repositories (e.g., Github). Therefore, CVE does not provide enough information to get an overview of the status and evolution of existing vulnerabilities in the different software repositories and package managers.

The goal of this work is to study the open research problem of mapping CVE entries to open-source projects. To do so, we focus on the following contributions:

- We provide an overview of the landscape of open-source projects and libraries in popular package managers.
- We discuss and implement three concrete approaches to map CVE entries to open-source projects.
- We perform a frequency analysis of CVE entries corresponding to open-source packages based on the mapping approaches.
- Eventually, we discuss identified challenges and quality issues wrt. the available data and the mapping.

---

[1] https://www.synopsys.com/software-integrity/resources/analyst-reports/open-source-security-risk-analysis.html, last accessed 2023-02-09.

[2] https://heartbleed.com/, last accessed 2022-12-06.

[3] http://cve.mitre.org, last accessed 2023-02-09.

T. Dam (✉) · S. Neumaier
St. Pölten University of Applied Sciences, Pölten, Austria
e-mail: tobias.dam@fhstp.ac.at

S. Neumaier
e-mail: sebastian.neumaier@fhstp.ac.at

© The Author(s), under exclusive license to Springer Nature Switzerland AG 2024
P. Haber et al. (eds.), *Data Science—Analytics and Applications*,
https://doi.org/10.1007/978-3-031-42171-6_2

Table 1 The left table lists the number of projects in the top-7 package managers and the middle table the top-7 licenses across all packages. The right table gives the number of versions published at repositories in 2015 and 2019, respectively

P.M.	Projects	Perc.
Go	1,818,666	39.45
NPM	1,275,082	27.66
Packagist	313,278	6.80
Pypi	231,690	5.03
NuGet	199,447	4.33
Maven	184,871	4.01
Ruby	161,608	3.51
Others	425,020	9.22

License	Count	Perc.
MIT	1,637,451	44.13
Apache-2.0	848,475	22.87
ISC	332,676	8.97
Other	298,626	8.05
BSD-3	140,806	3.80
GPL-3.0	63,890	1.72
MPL-2.0	51,517	1.39
Others	336822	9.08

P.M.	2015	2019
NPM	716,207	3,892,909
NuGet	210,929	614,774
Pypi	150,591	469,753
Packagist	233,643	334,059
Maven	326,089	144,813
Others	459,265	364,164

2   Related Work

The overview and analysis of the open-source landscape in this paper is based on Libraries.io [7]. Alternatively, there are various other works that monitor existing repositories and provide quality and popularity metrics. For instance, the PyDriller framework [9] is a tool to mine git-based software repositories. In this respect, the GHTorrent framework [4] collects and provides data for all public projects available on Github and therefore is a very comprehensive resource for analysis.

The detection and reporting of vulnerabilities and threats in open-source software has been the subject of extensive research for several years already [2, 3, 6]. In a recent paper, Tan et al. report the deployment of security patches on stable branches of open-source projects [10]. Similar to our approach, the authors map CVE entries based on the name of an open-source package. The approach is however based on manual investigation of the software packages and the mappings.

Most related to our mapping of CVE entries to libraries in open-source repositories is the work of Snyk.io[4] which provides a monitoring service to identify vulnerable packages and libraries. It consists of a detailed list of security reports for various repositories and contains information about the vulnerability, the name of the affected library, the versions of the library that are affected, etc. Similarly, the GitHub Advisory Database[5] is a list of CVEs and GitHub originated security reports and vulnerabilities of software available on the GitHub platform.

3   Open Source Landscape

In the context of this paper, open source refers to source code that is made available in online software repositories for use or modification. In this work, we make use of the monitoring project *Libraries.io* [7]: it monitors and crawls the meta-information of over 30 package managers and indexes data from over 5 million projects. Libraries.io provides the collected information as open data; in this paper we make use of the January 2020 dump of the Libraries.io data which is hosted on Zenodo [7].

As shown in Table 1, currently the largest package managers are the platforms of the Go programming language and the Node.js platform NPM. According to the 2020 data, the Go platform makes up even 39% of all projects indexed in Libraries.io by listing 1.8 million projects; NPM lists around 1.3 projects which amount to 28%. The *Others* category in the left table includes 25 other repositories which only sum up to 9% of all indexed projects. Note that the size of a package managers (i.e. the number of versions hosted) does not necessarily correlate with the impact of these managers. For instance, while the language Go has the most populous package manager, it has not been in the 10 most popular languages in the last years.[6]

The middle table lists the 7 most common licenses across all packages and repositories. The most popular license is the MIT License (44% of the projects), which is a permissive license, i.e. it imposes only very limited restrictions on reuse and is highly compatible with other open-source licenses.

---

[4] https://snyk.io/, last accessed 2023-02-09.

[5] https://github.com/advisories, last accessed 2023-02-09.

[6] https://octoverse.github.com/2022/top-programming-languages, last accessed 2023-03-20.

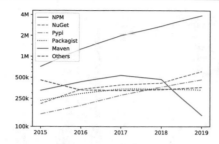

Fig. 1 Evolution of the total number of published versions at top-5 largest repositories; the y-axis is in logarithmic scale

Table 2 Number of new CVE entries in recent years

Year	CVE entries
2015	6,602
2016	6,520
2017	18,161
2018	18,213
2019	19,095
2020	20,516
2021	22,226

A version in the Libraries.io data corresponds to an immutable published version of a project from a repository. Table 1 (right) displays the number of versions published at the monitored repositories in 2015 and 2019, respectively. The largest repository NPM increased considerably from 716k to 3.9 million published versions per year. Figure 1 visualizes the rapid growth, in number of published versions, of the package managers NPM, NuGet, and PyPI.

4 Common Vulnerabilities and Exposures

In 1999, Mann and Christey [8] proposed the Common Vulnerability and Exposures (CVE) List, a public list of exposure references. The goal was to find out and document if multiple tools had identified the same vulnerabilities.

Each *CVE Identifier* in the list identifies a concrete vulnerability and gives an unique, individual name to it. New CVE identification numbers are assigned by the CVE Numbering Authorities (e.g., software vendors, open-source projects, security researchers). Table 2 displays the number of newly published CVE entries in the last 7 years. This number increased from 6.6k to 22.2k new entries.

Besides the ID and the summary of the vulnerability, a CVE entry provides relevant references (e.g., link to Github documentation), an assessment of the severity of the vulnerability using the Common Vulnerability Scoring System (CVSS), and the Common Weakness Enumeration (CWE) taxonomy of weakness types. Additionally, the CVE entry provides Common Platform Enumerations (CPE) [1] version 2.3 string, which is a standard for identifying classes of applications, operating systems/platforms, as well as hardware information. The CPE string consists of various fields providing information such as the software name, vendor as well as the target software, which contains the software computing environment (e.g. "node.js" or "python").

5 Findings

To perform this study, we use the most recent Open Data dump of the Libraries.io database[7] —available as compressed archive of several CSV files—to obtain data about open-source repositories and respective libraries; details of the repositories are described in Section 3. The Libraries.io data includes the fields NAME, PLATFORM (the package manager), ID, REPOSITORY TYPE (e.g., GitHub), REPOSITORY LINK, REPOSITORY OWNER and KEYWORDS.

---

[7] https://zenodo.org/record/3626071/files/libraries-1.6.0-2020-01-12.tar.gz, last accessed 2023-02-09.

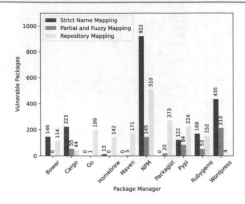

Fig. 2 Vulnerable package count of the top-10 package manager across all three mapping approaches

We used the dockerized version of the open-source project CVE-Search[8] as basis for our CVE analyses. The Computer Incident Response Center Luxembourg (CIRCL) operates a publicly accessible instance of the CVE-Search project and provides a daily dump of their CVE data in JSON format,[9] which we imported into our database. The CIRCLE CVE data provides the CVE fields SUMMARY and REFERENCES, as well as the fields PRODUCT and TARGET SOFTWARE which hold extracted information from the Common Platform Enumerations (CPE) information.

5.1   Mapping Approaches

In order to establish a mapping between the software packages of the Libraries.io dataset and the corresponding CVE entries of the CIRCL CVE dataset, we applied three different approaches, yielding varying results:

Strict Name Mapping The first approach iterates over each entry contained in the Libraries.io dataset and checks whether the package manager (in the field PLATFORM) can be matched to any target software in the CIRCL CVE dataset (as stated in the TARGET SOFTWARE field).

For our query, we created a mapping between package manager values of the Libraries.io dataset and the corresponding TARGET SOFTWARE values. The query then matches the value of the Libraries.io NAME field with the values of the CVE PRODUCT field as well as the PLATFORM value with either the TARGET SOFTWARE or checks if it is contained in the SUMMARY of the CVE dataset.

Discussion: The results of this mapping, i.e. the vulnerable package counts, is compared with the other matching approaches in Fig. 2. The figure is limited to the top-10 package managers wrt. number of mapped packages. The *strict name mapping* approach yields an unexpected low number of mapped packages for certain package managers. We identified the following issues: (i) In particular, Go packages provide the repository identifier consisting of provider, owner and repository name in the Libraries.io dump, while the CVE entry contains only the repository name. (ii) The CPE strings of CVE entries contain potentially wrong attribute values or lack some information as for instance the *target_sw* value. (iii) Additionally, various entries do not specify the package manager, neither in the CPE string nor inside the SUMMARY.

Additionally to comparing the amount of vulnerable packages, we grouped the CVE entries per year and package manager if we were able to create a mapping with the *strict name mapping* approach. This distribution as well as the trend of the top-7 package managers with the highest CVE count are depicted in Fig. 3. Despite some fluctuating values, there is a noticeable upwards trend especially for the last few years.

Partial and Fuzzy Name Matching In our second approach we build a lookup table for each package manager: we define specific keywords (e.g., NPM, Maven, etc.) for the CVE SUMMARY field and domain names or partial URLs (e.g., npmjs.com, pypi.org, etc.) for the REFERENCES. We iterate over each CVE entry, assign a package manager based on the lookup table,

---

[8] https://github.com/cve-search/cve-search, last accessed 2023-02-09.

[9] https://www.circl.lu/opendata/, last accessed 2023-02-09.

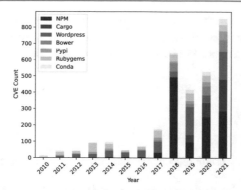

Fig. 3 Comparison of CVE count per package manager per year including seven package managers containing most entries

Table 3 The left table gives the top-5 vulnerable package count per package manager using the *repository matching* approach. "All Links" counts all packages with a matching link, "First Links" counts the first match. The right table gives the 10 most occurring repositories in the Libraries.io dataset

P.M.	All Links	First Link
Go	13201	199
NPM	5359	510
Maven	3396	171
Pypi	458	224
Ruby	432	152

Repository	Count
github.com/openshift/origin	1523
github.com/kubernetes/kubernetes	1181
github.com/liferay/liferay-portal	508
github.com/facebook/create-react-app	508
github.com/lodash/lodash	499

and check if the Libraries.io PLATFORM value equals the assigned package manager and if a value of the CVE PRODUCT list occurs either in the NAME or KEYWORDS fields. In case multiple Libraries.io entries match the CVE entry, our program uses a fuzzy string matching method provided by the fuzzyset2 python package[10] with a *cutoff* value of 0.3 and chooses the entry with the highest similarity value. This low cutoff value was empirically chosen since we observed a number of projects with matching substrings but mismatching content length and surroundings.

Discussion: The results of this approach are shown in Fig. 2. The vulnerable package counts of the *partial and fuzzy name matching* are considerably lower than compared to the strict name mapping approach. Due to choosing the best result of the fuzzy string matching as well as the necessary *cutoff* to avoid high false-positive rates, the approach is prone (i) to miss sub-packages with the same package name and (ii) to miss matches because of the *cutoff* value.

Repository Matching In order to increase the accuracy of the matching of software packages to CVE entries, we focus in this approach on the references in the respective CVE entries. The hypothesis is that the URLs in the references consist of the repository owner and repository name.[11]

We use the value of the Libraries.io REPOSITORY URL field and extract the repository provider (i.e., github.com, bit-bucket.org or gitlab.com) as well as the owner and the name of the repository. REPO_LINK contains the concatenated values of those fields. Additionally, we search for partial URLs of the format *provider.tld/owner/repository* in the CVE REFERENCES fields and store the results in a new array LINKS.

We iterate over the CVE entries and check whether the values of the LINKS array occur in the REPO_LINK field of any Libraries.io entry. First, we assigned the CVE entries to every package that matched the repository link resulting in very different vulnerable package counts compared to the other approaches. These results are shown in the "All Links" column of Table 3. To determine the amount of multiply assigned CVE entries, we reapplied the approach and only counted the first match of the repository link. Notably, in the "First Link" column of Table 3, the vulnerable package count is considerably lower. Figure 2 compares the "First Link" results to the other matching methods.

---

[10] https://pypi.org/project/fuzzyset2, last accessed 2023-02-09.

[11] Consider for instance the GitHub URLs, which include the organisation/owner and repository.

Discussion: We found, that various entries in the Libraries.io dataset contain the same REPOSITORY URL or at least the same combination of repository provider, owner and repository name. A lot of them seem to be sub-packages that are contained inside one repository or they erroneously contain the URL of the main project. Table 3 shows the ten most common REPO_LINK values and the respective package count.

5.2   Identified Challenges

To summarize, we identified the following challenges when mapping CVE to open source packages:

1. *No clear repository identifiers:* The CVE entries do not contain clear identifiers of the code base in the package manager and/or software repository.
2. *Incomplete or wrong CVE entries:* The CVE list potentially contains wrong attribute values or lacks some critical information to map to code bases.
3. *Multiple relevant software packages:* In some cases, the CVE entry relates to multiple software packages and potentially multiple code repositories.
4. *Reliable datasets:* There is no complete and reliable index of open source projects; the Libraries.io data is potentially erroneous and incomplete.

The mapping approaches allowed us to derive some insights regarding the number of vulnerabilities for certain package managers (cf. Fig. 2), in particular, the strict name mapping approach displayed a noticeable upwards trend in reported vulnerabilities in recent years (Fig. 3), however, an improved approach and a thorough evaluation is necessary to reach robust conclusions.

6   Conclusion

In this work, we have provided insights in the landscape of open-source projects in popular package managers, and have discussed three approaches to map an up-to-date list of CVE entries to their respective software package. In our analyses we have discussed both, shortcomings and quality issues of the available data, and shortcomings of the mapping wrt. accuracy and false-positive rate.

In future work, we plan the following research directions: Firstly, a thorough evaluation of the mapping approaches is required to provide more accurate results and to provide a large-scale mapping of CVE entries. Second, performing data cleansing on the Libraries.io and the CVE dataset would highly increase accuracy and would enable further analyses about software packages and their vulnerabilities. Third, research in improving the CVE standard; adding for instance additional meta-information such as a project identifier or project URL.

Another possibility to improve our work is to consider alternative data sources, such as the GHTorrent [5] database—a large and rich (meta)database of GitHub projects—as an additional DB to map with.

Acknowledgements This research was funded by the Austrian Research Promotion Agency (FFG) Bridge project 880592 "SecDM—Sichere und vertrauens-würdige on-premise data markets". The financial support by the Austrian Research Promotion Agency is gratefully acknowledged. We are grateful to the anonymous referees for suggesting numerous improvements.

References

1. Cheikes, B.A., Cheikes, B.A., Kent, K.A., Waltermire, D.: Common platform enumeration: naming specification version 2.3. US Department of Commerce, National Institute of Standards and Technology (2011)
2. Decan, A., Mens, T., Constantinou, E.: On the impact of security vulnerabilities in the npm package dependency network. In: 15th International Conference on Mining Software Repositories, MSR 2018. ACM (2018). https://doi.org/10.1145/3196398.3196401
3. Edwards, N., Chen, L.: An historical examination of open source releases and their vulnerabilities. In: The ACM Conference on Computer and Communications Security, CCS'12, pp. 183–194. ACM (2012). https://doi.org/10.1145/2382196.2382218
4. Gousios, G.: The ghtorent dataset and tool suite. In: 2013 10th Working Conference on Mining Software Repositories (MSR), pp. 233–236. IEEE (2013)

5. Gousios, G., Vasilescu, B., Serebrenik, A., Zaidman, A.: Lean ghtorrent: Github data on demand. In: Proceedings of the 11th Working Conference on Mining Software Repositories, pp. 384–387 (2014)
6. Kaplan, B., Qian, J.: A survey on common threats in npm and pypi registries. CoRR **abs/2108.09576** (2021). https://arxiv.org/abs/2108.09576
7. Katz, J.: Libraries.io Open Source Repository and Dependency Metadata (Jan 2020). https://doi.org/10.5281/zenodo.3626071
8. Mann, D.E., Christey, S.M.: Towards a common enumeration of vulnerabilities. In: 2nd Workshop on Research with Security Vulnerability Databases, Indiana (1999)
9. Spadini, D., Aniche, M., Bacchelli, A.: Pydriller: Python framework for mining software repositories. In: Proceedings of the 2018 26th ACM Joint Meeting on European Software Engineering Conference and Symposium on the Foundations of Software Engineering, pp. 908–911. ACM (10 2018). https://doi.org/10.1145/3236024.3264598
10. Tan, X., Zhang, Y., Cao, J., Sun, K., Zhang, M., Yang, M.: Understanding the practice of security patch management across multiple branches in oss projects. In: ACM Web Conference (2022). https://doi.org/10.1145/3485447.3512236

CSRX: A Novel Crossover Operator for a Genetic Algorithm Applied to the Traveling Salesperson Problem

Martin Uray iD, Stefan Wintersteller, and Stefan Huber iD

Abstract In this paper, we revisit the application of Genetic Algorithm (GA) to the Traveling Salesperson Problem (TSP) and introduce a family of novel crossover operators that outperform the previous state of the art. The novel crossover operators aim to exploit symmetries in the solution space, which allows us to more effectively preserve well-performing individuals, namely the fitness invariance to circular shifts and reversals of solutions. These symmetries are general and not limited to or tailored to TSP specifically.

Keywords Genetic algorithm · Traveling salesperson problem · Crossover operator

1   Introduction

Given n points in the plane, the Traveling Salesperson Problem (TSP) asks for the shortest closed tour that visits all points. It is a classical optimization problem and known to be NP-complete. Consequently, besides approximately optimal algorithms of polynomial complexity (PTAS), it is also a natural candidate for all kinds of optimization methods in Artificial Intelligence (AI). In particular, essentially the entire palette of meta-heuristic methods has been thoroughly studied for TSP, including Genetic Algorithm (GA) [9].

GA is used for optimization and search tasks and is inspired by natural selection in evolution. Given a set of candidate solutions, fit individuals are selected and recombined to form fitter offsprings, such that a population of individuals evolves over time from generation to generation. The recombination happens by means of a so-called crossover operator [12].

In 2021, the first competition on solving the TSP was organized. This competition focused on the application of surrogate-based optimization and Deep Reinforcement Learning. For an overview of the literature on both domains, including an overview of the application of Deep Neural Networks, as well as a description of the competing methods, the reader may be referred to [2].

Gog and Chira [6] introduced the Best Order Crossover (BOX), a crossover operator extending the well-established Order Crossover (OX) [3]. The OXs intended application are order-based problems. For crossing over two parents, the OX chooses two random splitting points within the first parent and copies the enclosed strings into the first offspring. The remaining numbers are then inserted in the order they appear in the second parent. On the other hand, the BOX operator incorporates the knowledge about the global best individual to generate a new offspring. By using random splitting points and assigning each a value, the offspring is generated by using the numbers from the first parent, defined by the order of the segments of the second parent and the global best. In the comparative study [6], the BOX outperforms all other operators. To the best of the authors knowledge, no other study outperformed this operator on the classical, vanilla TSP.

M. Uray · S. Huber
Josef Ressel Centre for Intelligent and Secure Industrial Automation, Salzburg University of Applied Sciences, Salzburg, Austria
e-mail: stefan.huber@fh-salzburg.ac.at

M. Uray (✉) · S. Wintersteller · S. Huber
Department for Information Technologies and Digitalisation, Salzburg University of Applied Sciences, Salzburg, Austria
e-mail: martin.uray@fh-salzburg.ac.at

S. Wintersteller
e-mail: swintersteller.its-m2020@fh-salzburg.ac.at

P. Haber et al. (eds.), *Data Science—Analytics and Applications*,
https://doi.org/10.1007/978-3-031-42171-6_3

In recent years, the interest of the research community shifted towards more general variants of the TSP. For this, special variants are possible, and adaptions of the GA were proposed to solve, among others, large-scale colored TSP [4], or real-life oriented multiple TSP [8]. Crossover operators tailored for the TSP are introduced for multiparent [11] and multi-offspring [13] setups. Based on the cycle crossover, a modified cycle crossover operator is introduced for the application with the TSP [7]. A more comprehensive overview of the GA applied to the TSP is given by Osaba et al. [9]. There, the most notable crossover variants for the TSP are being discussed.

We observe that TSP possesses certain symmetry properties. However, well-known crossover operators do not respect these and, as a consequence, fail to produce fit offsprings from fit parents. Following this observation, we present a novel family of crossover operators that are designed to respect these symmetries and demonstrate that our novel crossover operators significantly outperform the previous state of the art. Since the symmetries we exploit are of general nature, our methodology is of general interest and not limited to TSP specifically.

2   Background

2.1   Traveling Salesperson Problem (TSP)

Informally, TSP asks for the shortest, closed path that visits a given set of n locations exactly once. Note that we can reduce TSP to find the optimal order of the locations $p_0, \ldots, p_{n-1}$ that yields the shortest length of the resulting tour.

To encompass a large variety of applications, we can formalize TSP as follows: Given $p_0, \ldots, p_{n-1}$ in a metric space (X, d) with a metric d, encode a tour as a permutation $\pi : \{0, \ldots, n-1\} \to \{0, \ldots, n-1\}$ and ask for a tour π that minimizes the tour length $\ell(\pi)$ with

$$\ell(\pi) = \sum_{i=0}^{n-1} d(p_{\pi(i)}, p_{\pi((i+1) \bmod n)}). \tag{1}$$

In this paper, we may interchangeably represent a permutation π as the sequence $(\pi(0), \ldots, \pi(n-1))$, when it fits better to the formal setting.

A natural choice for d is the Euclidean metric, which we use for experiments in this paper. However, the discussed methods work with any metric. For instance, to optimize the commissioning sequence in high-bay storage, the movements in the vertical and horizontal direction may not happen simultaneously or at the same speed, which can be modeled by d accordingly, e.g., using the Manhattan metric or an affine transform of the Euclidean metric.

In literature, there is a special asymmetric variant of the TSP [1]. This variant is characterized by the property, that the distances have a different value, dependent on their traversal direction, i.e. where a tour $d(p_{\pi(i)}, p_{\pi(i+1)}) \neq d(p_{\pi(i+1)}, p_{\pi(i)})$. Nevertheless, in this work, we only consider the vanilla, symmetric TSP. For more details on the TSP, the reader is referred to [9].

2.2   Genetic Algorithm (GA)

The GA is an optimization and search procedure that is inspired by the maxim "survival of the fittest" in natural evolution. A candidate solution (individual) is encoded by a string (genetic code) over some alphabet. Individuals are modified by two genetic operators: (i) random alteration (mutation) of single individuals and (ii) recombination (crossover) of two (or more) parents to form offsprings. Given a set of individuals (population), a selection mechanism based on a fitness function together with the two genetic operators produce a sequence of populations (generations). The genetic operators promote the exploration of the search space while the selection mechanism attempts to promote the survival of fit individuals over generations.

For GA to work well, it is paramount that a suitable genetic representation of individuals is used. In particular, the crossover operator needs to have the property that the recombination of the genetic codes of two fit parents produces fit offsprings again, otherwise, the genetic structure of fit individuals would not survive over generations, and GA easily degenerates to a randomized search. (We shall also note that the crossover operator also needs to produce valid genetic encodings of individuals, e.g., encodings of permutations for TSP.) For more details on the GA, the reader is referred to [12, Chap. 4].

For TSP, it is common to take the sequence $(\pi(0), \ldots, \pi(n-1))$ of a permutation π as the genetic code and $-\ell(\pi)$ would be the fitness of π. The so-called one-point crossover operator works as follows for TSP. It takes two parents π_1 and π_2, chooses a random split index $0 \leq s < n$, and produces an offspring $\pi_1 \times_s \pi_2$ as follows: It takes the prefix $(\pi_1(0), \ldots, \pi_1(s))$

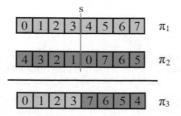

Fig. 1 The recombination of π_1 and π_2 into an offspring π_3 using CSX

of π_1 and fills up the remaining entries in the order as they occur in π_2, to form a permutation $\pi_1 \times_s \pi_2$. This way the "genetic information" of both parents is recombined. For instance, let $\pi_1 = (0, \ldots, 7)$ and $\pi_2 = (7, \ldots, 0)$ and let $s = 3$. Then $\pi_1 \times_3 \pi_2 = (0, 1, 2, 3, 7, 6, 5, 4)$. Besides this elementary crossover operator, there are many more. We refer to [6] for comparison for TSP.

3   Novel Crossover Operators Exploiting Symmetry

Let us again consider the example of $\pi_1 \times_s \pi_2$ and let us assume that π_1 was a fit individual, or for the sake of argument, let us assume that π_1 is indeed optimal. Observe that π_2 is the reversed version of π_1, which we denote by π_1^*, and hence has the same fitness. Though π_1 might be optimal, $\pi_1 \times_s \pi_1^*$ is in general far from optimal, since we first traverse π_1 and after index s we reverse direction due to π_1^*. A similar situation happens when π_2 is a circularly shifted version of π_1. We observe that the one-point crossover operator is ignorant of the symmetries of TSP, and so are all crossover operators reviewed in [6]. This, however, impairs the preservation of fit solutions or substructures over generations.

From a more algebraic point of view, let us denote by Π the set of all permutations of $\{0, \ldots, n-1\}$. Note that TSP possesses the following symmetry properties: A permutation $\pi \in \Pi$ or its reversed counterpart, or circular shifts of either, are essentially the same solutions, not the least according to the fitness. Let us denote by $\equiv$ the corresponding equivalence relation over Π, i.e., $\pi \equiv \pi'$ if they are the same modulo reversing and circular shifting. So instead of GA to act on the original space Π, we want to act on the smaller quotient space $\Pi/\equiv$, which more concisely captures the problem TSP.

More precisely, we want a new crossover operator $\overline{\times}$ that acts on $\Pi/\equiv$ in the following sense: If $\pi_1 \equiv \pi_1'$ and $\pi_2 \equiv \pi_2'$ then we also want $\pi_1 \overline{\times} \pi_2 \equiv \pi_1' \overline{\times} \pi_2'$. That is, $\overline{\times}$ agrees with $\equiv$ and we can think of $\overline{\times}$ acting on congruence classes of $\equiv$, e.g., $[\pi_1]_\equiv \overline{\times} [\pi_2]_\equiv$ is justified as notation.

We achieve this by, in some sense, factoring out circular shifts and reversals of individuals during the crossover. When we factor out the circular shifts for the one-point crossover operator, we call this the Circular Shift Crossover (CSX) operator. When we factor circular shifts and reversals, we call this the Circular Shift Reversal Crossover (CSRX) operator. The Reversal Crossover (RX) operator, we introduced in a preliminary work in [14], can be interpreted as factoring out reversals from the one-point crossover operator. However, in general, this technique can be applied to all kinds of existing crossover operators, including BOX, which is the current state of the art [6].

In more detail, CSX works as follows: Let us consider π_1 and π_2 and choose a split index s. Now circularly shift π_2 such that $\pi_2(s) = \pi_1(s)$ and apply the ordinary one-point crossover. See Fig. 1 for an example.

For RX we face the obstacle that we cannot "normalize" the traversal direction of a tour π in a natural way. That is, we cannot tell directly whether π_2 or its reversal π_2^* is "compatible" with π_1. So we let the fitness $-\ell$ decide: We consider both candidates and their fitness for the one-point crossover, $\ell(\pi_1 \times_s \pi_2)$ and $\ell(\pi_1 \times_s \pi_2^*)$, and take the one with the better fitness, i.e. the shorter tour length. This way we get invariant of the traversal direction of π_2, and this is what we aim for from the algebraic point of view from above. For CSRX we combine both strategies, i.e., we apply CSX to combine π_1 with π_2 and π_2^* and take the one with the better fitness. See Fig. 2 for an example. Note that π_2 is a reversed and circularly shifted version of π_1 in Fig. 2 and π_1 is restored in Fig. 2b. That is, if π_1 was optimal then CSRX again yields an optimal individual.

4   Experimental Evaluation

Setup. For all the experiments in this work, a common setup is established. As there are already libraries for standard implementations of the GA algorithm, we do not implement the algorithms from scratch, rather we use a library called

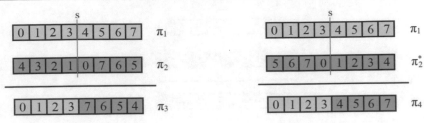

(a) π_1 and π_2 recombined to candidate state π_3 using CSX.

(b) π_1 and π_2^* recombined to candidate state π_4 using CSX.

Fig. 2 Recombination of π_1 and π_2 to candidates π_3 and π_4 for CSRX

Table 1 Experimental results after 1000 generations

Data set	OPT	BOX(orig)	BOX(reimp)	CSRX	Δ_{rel}^{BOX}	Δ_{rel}^{CSRX}
att48	33523	n/a	35872 ($\pm$806)	34789 ($\pm$488)	7.00%	3.77%
eil51	426	460	460 ($\pm$9)	442 ($\pm$5)	7.98%	3.75%
st70	675	741	818 ($\pm$24)	708 ($\pm$15)	21.19%	4.88%

mlrose[1] as a basis and improve the above stated algorithm based on this library. This library already provides a mapping of the TSP to a set of implementations of well-known AI methods, which makes it a favorable candidate for our experiments.

The proposed CSRX is challenged against BOX, which was the best performing crossover operator on TSP as reported in [6] and we follow the implementation details given in [6].

The experiments are evaluated on three different standard data sets for TSP: *att48*, *eil51* and *st70*. All three are included in the TSPLIB [10]. The data set *att48* contains 48 cities in a coordinate system with a known Optimal Tour Length (OPT) of 33523. The *eil51* data set has 51 cities with an OPT of 426, and the *st70* data set has 70 cities and an OPT of 675.

Results. All experiments are configured using a shared parameter set, with a population size of 100 and a mutation rate of 0.05 as defined in the reference paper [6]. An inversion-mutation is implemented as a mutation strategy [5].

The first experiment uses a maximum number of 1000 generations. To ensure more reliable results, the experiments were repeated 10 times with different seeds.

A common strategy to not lose good solutions, to add elitism, i.e. to keep a certain number of the fittest individuals for the next generation. The original paper does not specify how exactly the elitism is configured. However, our experiments show that an elitism size of 10% performs the best using a grid search for the set parameter configurations ([0%, 1%, 10%, 20%, 30%]), and showed the highest convergence to the numbers presented in [6].

The results of this first experiment can be seen in Table 1. This table illustrated the numbers (mean $\pm$ std) from the original paper (BOX(orig)), the numbers from our reimplementation (BOX(reimp)), and the introduced CSRX operator, accompanied by the optimal tour length (OPT). Since the referenced paper [6] did not evaluate the BOX operator towards the *att48* data set, no numbers are available. We denote the relative error of the reimplemented version of BOX by $\Delta_{rel}^{BOX} = \frac{BOX-OPT}{OPT}$, and Δ_{rel}^{CSRX} analogously for CSRX.

As can be seen in Table 1, the reported numbers of BOX(orig) could not be reproduced exactly for the *st70* data set.[2] Even if this single number diverges, it can be seen that the introduced CSRX operator outperforms both, BOX(orig) and BOX(reimp). On the *att48*, *eil51*, and *st70* data sets, difference of the relative error ($\Delta_{rel}^{BOX} - \Delta_{rel}^{CSRX}$) of 3.23%, 4.23%, and 16.29% are observed, respectively. On all three data sets, the CSRX operator has a much lower standard deviation. Figure 3 shows the results over the course of the 1000 generations.

As can be clearly seen in Fig. 3, the CSRX operator is outperforming the BOX operator already within the first 200 generations. Based on this fact, the results for the following experiment are bootstrapped: we reduce the computational costs of our experiments by decreasing the number of generations to 200 in the following. In turn, the number of experiments conducted has been raised to 100.

---

[1] https://mlrose.readthedocs.io/.

[2] This issue was brought to the attention of the authors of the reference. We contacted the authors, but no response was received at the point of submission.

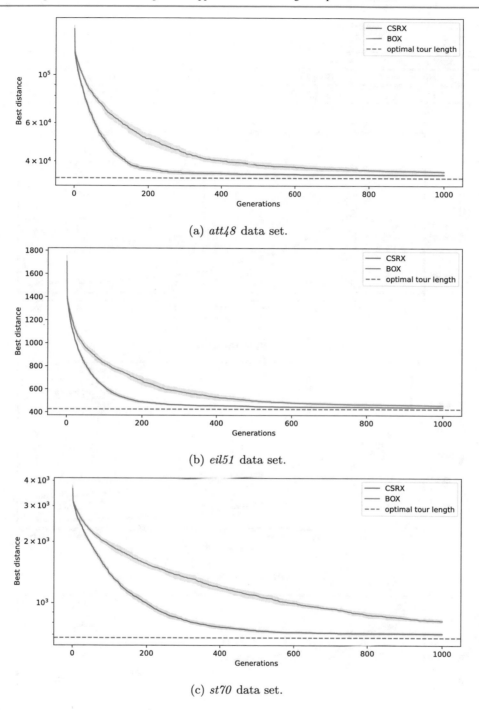

(a) *att48* data set.

(b) *eil51* data set.

(c) *st70* data set.

Fig. 3 The results on a 95% confidence interval. BOX(reimp) compared with CSRX on 1000 Generations on the three data sets. This experiment replicates the results from [6]

For this setup, an elitism of 20% empirically performs best on both, the CSRX and the BOX. Also here, the same search space, as in the previous experiment was used and evaluated using a grid search. The results of this experiment can be seen in Table 2 and Fig. 4, numerically and visually over the number of generations, respectively. Also, these results show, that the introduced CSRX operator outperforms the BOX operator. The difference in the relative error on the three data sets is 39.38%, 42.25%, and 83.40% for the data sets *att48*, *eil51*, and *st70*, respectively. Also here, the standard deviation is significantly lower, compared to the BOX.

Table 2 Experimental results after 200 generations

Data set	OPT	BOX(reimp)	CSRX	Δ_{rel}^{BOX}	Δ_{rel}^{CSRX}
att48	33523	50033 ($\pm$3648)	36830 ($\pm$1233)	49.25%	9.86%
eil51	426	655 ($\pm$39)	475 ($\pm$15)	53.76%	11.50%
st70	675	1484 ($\pm$85)	921 ($\pm$46)	119.85%	36.44%

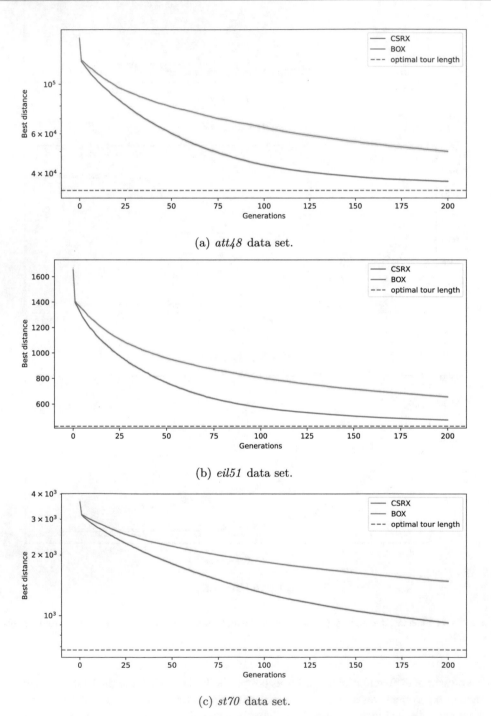

(a) *att48* data set.

(b) *eil51* data set.

(c) *st70* data set.

Fig. 4 The second experiment on a 95% confidence interval. The BOX(reimp) compared with CSRX on 200 Generations on the three data sets

5 Conclusion

In this paper, we introduced a new technique of general nature on how to facilitate crossover operators, aiming to improve GA on the task of the TSP. These techniques utilize the symmetry properties of the optimization problem so that two fit parents will not be steered to generate unfit offsprings.

Furthermore, we used these proposed techniques to facilitate a very simple one-point crossover to demonstrate their abilities and received the CSRX operator. In an experimental evaluation against the best performing crossover operator for the TSP in the latest comparative study [6], the BOX, the CSRX clearly outperformed on all given tasks. In future work, we plan to transfer our technique to BOX.

References

1. Asadpour, A., Goemans, M.X., Mǎdry, A., Gharan, S.O., Saberi, A.: An O log n/Log Log n-approximation algorithm for the asymmetric traveling salesman problem. Oper. Res. **65**(4), 1043–1061 (2017). https://doi.org/10.5555/3216622.3216635
2. Bliek, L., da Costa, P., Refaei Afshar, R., Zhang, Y., Catshoek, T., Vos, D., Verwer, S., Schmitt-Ulms, F., Hottung, A., Shah, T., Sellmann, M., Tierney, K., Perreault-Lafleur, C., Leboeuf, C., Bobbio, F., Pepin, J., Silva, W., Gama, R., Fernandes, H., Zaefferer, M., López-Ibáñez, M., Irurozki, E.: The First AI4TSP Competition: Learning to Solve Stochastic Routing Problems (2022). http://arxiv.org/abs/2201.10453
3. Davis, L. (ed.): Handbook of Genetic Algorithms. Van Nostrand Reinhold, New York, NY (1991)
4. Dong, X., Cai, Y.: A novel genetic algorithm for large scale colored balanced traveling salesman problem. Future Gen. Comput. Syst. **95**, 727–742 (2019). https://doi.org/10.1016/j.future.2018.12.065
5. Fogel, D.B.: Applying evolutionary programming to selected traveling salesman problems. Cybern. Syst. **24**(1), 27–36 (1993). https://doi.org/10.1080/01969729308961697
6. Gog, A., Chira, C.: Comparative analysis of recombination operators in genetic algorithms for the travelling salesman problem. In: Corchado, E., Kurzyński, M., Woźniak, M. (eds.) Hybrid Artificial Intelligent Systems, Lecture Notes in Computer Science, vol. 6679, pp. 10–17. Springer, Berlin (2011). https://doi.org/10.1007/978-3-642-21222-2_2
7. Hussain, A., Muhammad, Y.S., Nauman Sajid, M., Hussain, I., Mohamd Shoukry, A., Gani, S.: Genetic algorithm for traveling salesman problem with modified cycle crossover operator. Comput. Intell. Neurosci. **2017**, 1–7 (2017). https://doi.org/10.1155/2017/7430125
8. Lo, K.M., Yi, W.Y., Wong, P.K., Leung, K.S., Leung, Y., Mak, S.T.: A genetic algorithm with new local operators for multiple traveling salesman problems. Int. J. Comput. Intell. Syst. **11**(1), 692–705 (2018). https://doi.org/10.2991/ijcis.11.1.53
9. Osaba, E., Yang, X.S., Del Ser, J.: Traveling salesman problem: a perspective review of recent research and new results with bio-inspired metaheuristics. In: Yang, X.S. (ed.) Nature-Inspired Computation and Swarm Intelligence, pp. 135–164. Elsevier (2020). https://doi.org/10.1016/B978-0-12-819714-1.00020-8
10. Reinelt, G.: TSPLIB-a traveling salesman problem library. ORSA J. Comput. **3**(4), 376–384 (1991). https://doi.org/10.1287/ijoc.3.4.376
11. Roy, A., Manna, A., Maity, S.: A novel memetic genetic algorithm for solving traveling salesman problem based on multi-parent crossover technique. Decis. Making: Appl. Manage. Eng. **2**(2), 100–111 (2019). https://doi.org/10.31181/dmame1902076r
12. Russell, S.J., Norvig, P.: Artificial Intelligence: A Modern Approach. Pearson Series in Artificial Intelligence, 4th edn. Pearson, Hoboken (2021)
13. Wang, J., Ersoy, O.K., He, M., Wang, F.: Multi-offspring genetic algorithm and its application to the traveling salesman problem. Appl. Soft Comput. **43**, 415–423 (2016). https://doi.org/10.1016/j.asoc.2016.02.021
14. Wintersteller, S., Uray, M., Lehenauer, M., Huber, S.: Improvements for mlrose applied to the traveling salesperson problem. In: Moreno-Díaz, R., Pichler, F., Quesada-Arencibia, A. (eds.) Computer Aided Systems Theory—EUROCAST 2022, pp. 611–618. Springer Nature Switzerland, Cham, Switzerland (2022). https://doi.org/10.1007/978-3-031-25312-6_72

First Insight into Social Media User Sentiment Spreading Potential to Enhance the Conceptual Model for Disinformation Detection

Dino Pitoski[iD], Slobodan Beliga[iD], and Ana Meštrović[iD]

Abstract The networks of digital communication, including social media, have become the primary means for information dissemination. While these networks offer vast benefits, such as fast knowledge exchange, improved integration, as well as entertainment for their users, they also carry many negative aspects, such as the spread of false news and malicious content. In this paper, we propose the Sentiment Spread Potential (SSP) algorithm, which combines sentiment and temporal network analysis to calculate a user's potential for spreading information of different sentiment. This algorithm should be useful in the process of disinformation detection in the part of user profiling.

Keywords Social network analysis · Sentiment analysis · Temporal networks · Spreading potential

1 Introduction

The networks of digital communication, whose large part constitute the increasingly represented "social media networks", become the mainstream means for the exchange of information [1, 2]. Via these networks, which notably get established through means of websites, mobile applications, blogs, emails, live chats, web calling, and several additional infrastructure categories [3], the sharing of data and information, to subsequently acquire knowledge and wisdom [4], takes place with ever greater speed.

Apart from these, and the associated positive aspects they entice, such as the faster economic progress, or–simplistically put–the entertainment for their users, the networks of digital communication, due to the rapid spread of false news (mis-/dis- information) and malicious content (malinformation),[1] are increasingly perceived as dangerous [6]. Adding to this the increased isolation of individuals, the erosion of privacy, and other considerable problems that they entail [7, 8], the negative aspects of the exchange via digital communication networks can easily be perceived as to be overshadowing the benefits of an integrated society they enable.

This research is related to our previous studies that explored various aspects of information spreading and communication on Twitter, [9–11]. In [9] we studied how the tweet content can influence the spreading of tweets (in terms of retweeting), in [10] we used graph neural networks for retweet prediction, while in [11] we implemented and evaluated machine learning models for retweet classification combining content and network-based measures. We have performed extensive experiments within tasks related to detecting sentiment polarity of texts as well, mainly in the domain of COVID-19 related research [9, 12–14]. Thus, we have already gained considerable insights into how sentiment polarity, content, and network properties, may affect the information spreading on social media. With this study we go a step further, and propose a novel tool for aiding the disinformation detection on digital communication networks, based on measuring the sentiment spreading potential. We focus on user profiling as one of the tools used to assess the potential for the spread of disinformation. The underlying

---

[1]For one general distinction between the terms mis- and dis- information, as well as malinformation, as the main components of information disorder, see., e.g., [5]. For simplicity of language, throughout the text we will continue to use the term "disinformation" for the concept as a whole.

D. Pitoski (✉) · S. Beliga · A. Meštrović
Center for Artificial Intelligence and Cybersecurity, University of Rijeka, Rijeka, Croatia
e-mail: dino.pitoski@uniri.hr

S. Beliga · A. Meštrović
Faculty of Informatics and Digital Technologies, University of Rijeka, Rijeka, Croatia

© The Author(s), under exclusive license to Springer Nature Switzerland AG 2024
P. Haber et al. (eds.), *Data Science—Analytics and Applications*,
https://doi.org/10.1007/978-3-031-42171-6_4

concept–the temporal network node centrality indicator named "Spread Potential"–has been conceived in our forthcoming study [15].

More on the motivations and the related work is provided in next section, followed by the proposed methodology for the calculation of Sentiment Spread Potential of digital communication networks' users, in Sect. 3. We close this article with a discussion, in Sect. 4.

2   On the Information Disorder and the Benefits of Sentiment and Temporal Network Analysis

The issue of "fakeness" of news is inherently related to the issue of sentiment of the news' texts in general, as positive and negative experiences can be used as strategic instruments that affect political, economic, and other aforementioned conditions. The connection between these two concepts is in the notion that the fake news are positive or negative extremes of the text of the news of positive or negative sentiment polarity, if we understand the sentiment of the text as the intention to influence the aforementioned conditions. From a psychological perspective, this refers to promoting one's own commitment or belonging to a specific group with regard to group polarization (see, e.g., [16]). As one studied example, [17] show that ads sent through Facebook include intentionally placed specific sentiments at unique moments of the campaign for the 2016 US presidential elections, with the purpose of influencing the elections. The sentiment of the text in this example serves to guide users of digital communication platforms to encourage commitment to a certain group pole, which is almost equal to the achieved polarization. Recently it has been demonstrated empirically, by "planting" invented fake news samples, that polarization, and actually ideological segregation in general, will structurally increase the spread of false information across a social network, in a way that ideologically aligned news, which otherwise would be too implausible to propagate, become believable to biased partisans [18].

Some of the widely used complementary methods to the qualitative fact-checking performed by checking organizations (see, e.g., https://www.poynter.org/ifcn/) are the semi-automated text classifications, such as sentiment analyses of the news' texts. Sentiment analysis is a part of the field of natural language processing (NLP), which determines the level of positivity or negativity expressed in the information, the level of sensationalism in language used, as well as the level of excitement of the users of the information passed through digital communication networks, which can all be a signal that the information being shared is false or problematic in some way. Disinformation in news are often driven by short headlines with a strong excitement effect (mostly promoted through so-called clickbait), which can be marked by the strength of sentiment or excitement effect [19]. Some scholars go that far to hypothesize that when posing allegations against someone, or when giving a false statement about someone, the sentiment of the statements is generally negative [20].

Overall, the applications of sentiment analysis in detecting fake news are still relatively underrepresented in research, due to high chances of prejudice in interpreting the results, as well as due to technical problems such as multilingualism and multimodality [19]. Moreover, the "analysis of source", i.e., profiling the users in the networks of digital communication in fake news detection, is a method still emerging [21].

Meanwhile, the analysis of complex networks becomes a fundamental method for researching the *spread(ers)* of information across digital communication networks [22], and network science is one of the most promising scientific fields in general, as many phenomena, particularly social phenomena, can be observed as networks, with nodes (e.g., people) and links (interactions) between them [23]. At the same time, the field is relatively scarce in analysing and theorizing dynamic (temporal) networks; measures, indicators, algorithms and visualizations used in the analysis of complex networks are mostly reduced to binary and static abstractions of networks from data [24]. The spread of information across digital communication networks inevitably imposes drawing abstractions of temporal networks, as the temporal component is very important; one desires to trace *who* spreads, but also *how fast*, and *deep*, the *positive* or *negative* (or fake) information? Studies that develop indicators for dynamic networks exist [25–27], also there are some examples where sentiment analysis has been used in the combination with static network analysis (see [28], for example), but none, to our knowledge, has been committed to temporal network evaluations, especially combining it with sentiment valencing.

Against the overview of issues and methods provided above, in the sequel we provide our indicator methodology.

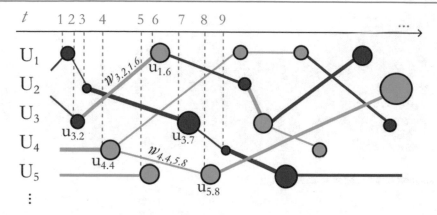

Fig. 1 **Simplified temporal network of digital communication**. U–users, t–time, w–weights based on sentiments; red (green) links and nodes represent negative (positive) sentiment for the contents transmitted

3 Methodology for Measuring the Sentiment Spread Potential of Digital Communication Networks' Users

Our methodology is underlain by the idea that an overall negative (positive) attitude profile of users relates in some consistent way to the speed and size of spread of negative (positive) news. In a temporal network we envisage user accounts (which include individual social media accounts such as those of Twitter, Facebook and Instagram users, as well as website and news portals' holders) as a set of nodes in which each node represents an aggregation of the user and the message annotated with a timestamp. The exchange of information between users at particular time points makes a directed (sender-to-recipient) link, with link weights being the overall valences of the message sentiments. The link weight ranges from -1 (highly negative) to 1 (highly positive). The method for deriving these valences can be any of the supervised, unsupervised, or combined methods for sentiment classification; in the conceptualization of the methodology unfolding, we take the polarity value of the lexemes as envisaged by [29]. These polarity values (valences), should be derived by applying the algorithm on the full corpus of text or content exchanged through the analysed network before its abstraction.

In Fig. 1 we show a simplified visualization of an imagined temporal network of digital communication abstracted from a communication exchange taking place in a selected interval. Both nodes and links reflect the transmission/transmitted information contents between senders and recipients (users). One can imagine the green links/nodes being those contents with greater overall positive sentiment, and red links/nodes being the contents with greater negative sentiment. The colour and size of the links and nodes reflect the positivity/negativity of the content transmitted.[2] Link durations include the duration of physical transmission of the message content, and the duration of the recipients' processing of the content. One can imagine a Twitter, Facebook or Instagram post being reposted or commented on with added contents as that which makes a specific network path. However, in this general model, the node-respective sources (user accounts) that continuously forward the communication can also be static, in terms of them only placing contents on their user accounts (e.g., news portals only placing the news at their sites), which subsequently gets picked up and disseminated by other accounts. The same user account can also repost the same or extended content on their own account, and some contents may stop being spread completely in the selected interval of observation.

The notion of the weighted directed temporal network illustrated in Fig. 1 can be formalised as follows. Let $G = (U, L, W)$ be a graph where:

- U is a set of nodes $u_{k.i}$, where k represents a user and i represents a time stamp of action of sending out a communicated content (in fact, a node $u_{k.i}$ is an aggregation of user account denoted as U_k and communicated content posted in time i and $U = \cup_{k=1}^{x} U_k$, where x is the total number of users in the network),

---

[2] In the methodology we do not consider links of neutral sentiment as the polarity value of the lexemes obtained through the proposed sentiment evaluation model does not in any case derive a strict zero value. If that value by any other sentiment classification method occurs on links, we suggest substituting with smallest negative or positive value to ensure the existence of a link (weight) and thereby the existence of a network path that otherwise would be cut.

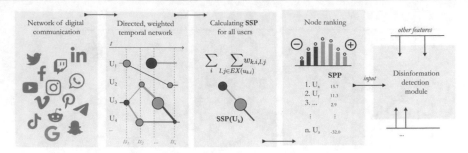

Fig. 2 Conceptual representation of the proposed methodology

- L is a set of links $l_{k.i,l.j}$ that connect sending and receiving nodes of the transmitted content, $u_{k.i}$ and $u_{l.j}$ between user accounts U_k and U_l, and
- W is a set of link weights $w_{k.i,l.j}$ assigned to the respective $l_{k.i,l.j}$, which weights are the calculated valences of the sentiment of the message content, ranging from -1 to 1.

Now, in such defined network, for each node observe all possible outgoing paths from an evaluated node $u_{k.i}$ to all other subsequent nodes in the graph. Let $EX(u_{k.i})$ be set of all paths outgoing from an evaluated node $u_{k.i}$ to all other $u_{l.j}$ where $ex_m(u_{k.i}) \in EX(u_{k.i})$ may not include the $l_{k.i,l.j}$ touching the same user account U_k as the one pertaining to node being evaluated, or to a node already traversed in the path.

The calculation of the algorithm that we name as "Sentiment Spread Potential" (SSP) of a user U_k, based on the previously defined parameters, is introduced by the following Equation:

$$SSP(U_k) = \sum_i \sum_{l.j \in EX(u_{k.i})} w_{k.i,l.j} \tag{1}$$

The application of the algorithm, which we provided for public use in our related work [15] via the following link: https://bit.ly/spreadpotential, is recommended as to be executed on the temporal networks abstracted from more than one representative interval of the same length taken from a wider time frame in which the analysed communication takes place. Upon the execution of the measure, the SSP ranks for each user for each interval for which it has been calculated would be averaged.

Also, when defining ex_ms one should be able to set the thresholds on when the the time is to short or too long for its content to be "picked up" by the subsequent user. In the available algorithm (the URL specified above) these thresholds are represented by variables "MIN_WAIT_TIME" and "MAX_WAIT_TIME" in the SP algorithm code refer to the transmission of content from one to the same user account (the variable named as "port" in the code). These time bounds, which are initialized in the code at 30 and 180 minutes are useful for one to be able to run sensitivity analyses (see the discussions in [15]). For the application in the case of digital communication networks as conceptualized in this article, these are recommended as to be set to zero and to infinity, respectively.

Ultimately, the SSP algorithm is offered as a feature in the task of disinformation detection, as it generates a rank list of the users by their influence. A recapitulation of the proposed methodology is offered with Fig. 2.

In the first stage, the digital communication is abstracted as a directed and weighted temporal network. Next, SSP is calculated for all users in the network according to Eq. 1. Using the computed SSP values, the nodes are ranked so that the most polarized values are on opposite sides (from the most positive extreme, over the neutral, to the most negative extreme). Spreading potential metadata is passed further to actors or components of the disinformation detection system, where it serves as a feature for identifying disinformation. More on the usability follows in next section.

4   Discussion and Conclusion

The above proposed algorithm, applied on the proposed temporal network abstraction, should serve as an indication of the potential of the digital communication participant (user) to spread any content in the analysed network relative to all other users, with this potential showing whether this user spreads content of a generally positive sentiment, or generally negative sentiment. As it incorporates the neighbour-of-neighbours connectedness, SSP comprises the sentiment influentiation of an individual user (account) on all other users in the network.

In these terms, our proposition is that SSP can serve to identify the high-probability spreader (top-ranked) nodes when it comes to positive or negative content they are prone to spread, which identification is one of the key steps in the process of detection of disinformation; user profiling.

Essentially, with SSP we compute the probability that a single user influences other users in the network to spread the information with the associated negative (positive) sentiment. Upon the algorithm application we obtain a list of users with the corresponding SSP values. At the top of the list are those users who have the greatest effect on others in terms of spreading contents of a positive/negative sentiment, and who may need to be monitored for disseminating or "planting" new disinformation when acting as a source. It is important to emphasize that in the calculation, not only the strength is counted in, but also the spreading speed and distance. In terms of speed, it follows from the fact that the measure is executed on a temporal abstraction; if there are many connections within the temporal network abstracted from the interval, the information to other nodes spreads faster. As regards the distance, this relates to the breadth and depth of the messaging between users; if there are more different users that are touched by any evaluated user, the distance that any message covers (this also relating to the concepts such as network density or diameter), is greater.

There are few points that need to be addressed regarding the envisaged methodology application. First, obviously the proposed concept needs further empirical validation. This should be done by planting some content in a real (physical) experimental network of users, similarly to what recently has been done by [18], to test whether there is a fit between the SSP ranking and the breadth and depth (and speed) of the spread of information.

Second, the mechanics of tracing the content spread via the communication networks needs to be established, in such way that the content that makes a temporal network path is credibly traced. Arguably, this can be done best by semi-automated assessment, i.e., several reviewers verifying computer results in terms of coding the transfer to the next account as it occured. Through this assessment the predetermined rules for the selection of the interval for the content spread, hence the rules for network abstraction, should be defined.

Third, the sentiment evaluation process for the content itself should be consistent, where sentiment designation methods may not vary within one and the same abstracted temporal network evaluated, while various other sentiment classification principles are recommended as to be tested for comparison (e.g., SentiStrength, see http://sentistrength.wlv.ac.uk/), including those by humans in manual coding.

With these points we conclude this conceptualization, which we intend to further validate by empirical testing (similar to the attempt made in [15], but on digital communication networks). We nevertheless encourage other researchers to test the algorithm on their case applications using the available definitions and the provided code.

Declarations

Authors' contributions

Conceptualization: D.P.; methodology: D.P.; validation: all authors; resources: all authors; writing-original draft preparation: all authors; writing-review and editing: all authors; visualization: all authors; project administration: D.P. and S.B.; funding acquisition: D.P. and S.B. All authors have read and agreed to the published version of the manuscript.

Funding

This research has been fully funded by the University of Rijeka, call "UNIRI Projects for Young Researchers and Artists" (2022), grant no(s): uniri-mladi-drustv-22-28 and uniri-mladi-drustv-22-39.

References

1. Chaffey, D.: Global social media statistics research summary 2022. In: Smart Insights Website (2022). https://www.smartinsights.com/social-media-marketing/social-media-strategy/new-global-social-mediaresearch/
2. Dixon, S.: Number of social media users worldwide from 2017 to 2027. In: Statista Website (2022). https://www.statista.com/statistics/278414/number-of-worldwide-social-network-users/
3. Epitech.: Digital communication: what is it? Concept and features. In: Epitech Website (2023). https://www.epitech-it.es/noticias-eventos/digital-communication-what-is-it/
4. Jennifer, R.: The wisdom hierarchy: representations of the DIKW hierarchy. J. Inf. Sci. 33(2), 163–180 (2007). https://doi.org/10.1177/0165551506070706
5. Claire, W., Hoda, D.: Information disorder: Toward an interdisciplinary framework for research and policymaking. Report No. DGI(2017)09, Strasbourg: Council of Europe (2017). https://rm.coe.int/information-disorder-towardan-interdisciplinary-framework-forresearc/168076277c
6. David, M.J., Lazer et al.: The science of fake news. Science 359(6380), 1094–1096 (2018). https://doi.org/10.1126/science.aao2998
7. Nancy, B.: Personal Connections in the Digital Age. Polity Press (2011). Isbn:9780745643323
8. Haidt, J., Twenge, J.: Social media and mental health: A collaborative review. In: Unpublished manuscript. https://tinyurl.com/SocialMediaMentalHealthReview
9. Karlo, B., et al.: Characterisation of COVID-19-related tweets in the Croatian language: framework based on the Cro-CoV-cseBERT model. Appl. Sci. 11(21), 10442 (2021)
10. Petrović, M., Hrelja, A., Meštrović, A.: Prediction of COVID- 19 tweeting: classification based on graph neural networks. In: 45th Jubilee International Convention on Information, Communication and Electronic Technology (MIPRO), pp. 307–311. IEEE (2022)
11. Meštrović, A., Petrović, M., Beliga, S.: Retweet prediction based on heterogeneous data sources: the combination of text and multilayer network features. Appl. Sci. 12(21), 11216 (2022)
12. Karlo, B., et al.: COVID-19-related communication on twitter: analysis of the croatian and polish attitudes. In: Proceedings of Sixth International Congress on Information and Communication Technology: ICICT 2021, vol. 3, pp. 379–390. Springer, London (2021)
13. Maja, B.P., et al.: Topic modelling and sentiment analysis of COVID-19 related news on Croatian Internet portal. In: Information Society 2020, pp. 5–9 (2020)
14. Ilić, A., Beliga, S.: The polarity of croatian online news related to COVID-19: a first insight. In: Central European Conference on Information and Intelligent Systems. Faculty of Organization and Informatics Varazdin, pp. 237–246 (2021)
15. Pitoski, D., Babić, K., Meštrović, A.: A new measure of node centrality on schedule-based space-time networks for the designation of spread potential. Submitted for publication to Scientific Reports, preprint available at Research Square (2023). https://assets.researchsquare.com/files/rs-2474713/v1/e026055f986e1ff332210102.pdf?c=1674017533
16. Van Wouter, A., et al.: Good news or bad news? conducting sentiment analysis on dutch text to distinguish between positive and negative relations. J. Inf. Technol. Politics 5(1), 73–94 (2008). https://doi.org/10.1080/19331680802154145
17. Alvarez, G., Choi, J., Strover, S.: Good news, bad news: a sentiment analysis of the 2016 election russian facebook ads. Int. J. Commun. 14, 3027–3053 (2020)
18. Jonas, S., Marc, K., van de Arnout, R.: Network segregation and the propagation of misinformation. Sci. Rep. 13(1), 917 (2023). https://doi.org/10.1038/s41598-022-26913-5
19. Alonso, M.A., et al.: Sentiment analysis for fake news detection. Electronics 10(11), 1348 (2021). https://doi.org/10.3390/electronics10111348
20. Bhavika, B., et al.: Fake news detection using sentiment analysis. In: 2019 3rd International Conference on Computing, Communication and Automation (ICCCA), pp. 1–5. IEEE (2019)
21. Liesbeth, A., Marie-Francine, M., Domenico, P.: Preventing profiling for ethical fake news detection. Inf. Process. Manage. 58(4), 103206 (2022). https://doi.org/10.1016/j.ipm.2022.103206
22. David, K., Jon, K., Éva, T.: Maximizing the spread of influence through a social network. In: Proceedings of the Ninth ACM SIGKDD International Conference on Knowledge Discovery and Data Mining, pp. 137–146. ACM (2003)
23. Ulrik, B., et al.: What is network science?". Network Sci. 1(01), 1–15 (2013). https://doi.org/10.1017/nws.2013.2
24. Dino, P., Thomas, J.L., Peter, P.: Human migration as a complex network: appropriate abstraction, and the feasibility of Network Science tools. In: Peter, H., et al. (eds.) Data Science–Analytics and Applications, pp. 113–120. Springer Fachmedien Wiesbaden, Wiesbaden (2021). Isbn:978-3-658-32182-6
25. Raj, K.P., Jari, S.: Path lengths, correlations, and centrality in temporal networks. Phys. Rev. E 84(1), 016105 (2011) https://doi.org/10.1103/PhysRevE.84.016105, www.link.aps.org/doi/101103/PhysRevE.84.016105
26. Hyoungshick, K., Ross, A.: Temporal node centrality in complex networks. Phys. Rev. E 85(2), 026107 (2012) https://doi.org/10.1103/PhysRevE.85.026107, www.link.aps.org/doi/10.1103/PhysRevE85.026107

27. Liu, C., Zhang, Z.-K.: Information spreading on dynamic social networks. Commun. Nonlinear Sci. Numer. Simul. **19**(4), 896–904 (2014). https://doi.org/10.1016/j.cnsns.2013.08.028
28. Bermingham, A., et al.: Combining social network analysis and sentiment analysis to explore the potential for online radicalisation. In: 2009 InFirst ternational Conference on Advances in Social Network Analysis and Mining (2009). https://doi.org/10.1109/ASONAM.2009.31
29. Tajana, B.K., Sanda, B.B., Benedikt, P.: Lexical sense labeling and sentiment potential analysis using corpus-based dependency graph. Mathematics **9**(12) (2021). Issn: 2227-7390. https://doi.org/10.3390/math9121449, https://www.mdpi.com/2227-7390/9/12/1449

Hateful Messages: A Conversational Data Set of Hate Speech Produced by Adolescents on Discord

Jan Fillies, Silvio Peikert, and Adrian Paschke

Abstract With the rise of social media, an increase of hateful content online can be observed. Even though the understanding and definitions of hate speech vary, platforms, communities, and legislature all acknowledge the challenge. Adolescents are a new and active group of social media users. The majority of adolescents experience or witness online hate speech. Research in the field of automated hate speech classification has been on the rise and focuses on aspects such as bias, generalizability, and performance. To increase generalizability and performance, it is important to understand biases within the data. This research addresses the bias of youth language within hate speech classification and contributes by providing a modern and anonymized hate speech youth language data set consisting of 88.395 annotated chat messages. The data set consists of publicly available online messages from the chat platform Discord. For 35.553 messages, the user profiles provided age annotations, setting the average author age to under 20 years old. 6,4% of the total messages were classified as hate speech using the annotation schema, which was adapted for this data set.

Keywords Hate speech · Youth language · Bias · Data set · NLP

1 Introduction

Research shows that there are differences within the language used by age groups online [16]. Most teenagers within the United States use social media [18]. Between January 2020 and March 2020 Facebook removed 9.6 million posts containing hate speech.[1] As of today, it is clear that social media is used often and frequently by adolescents. Hate speech and it's algorithmic detection has had an increasing interest in social media platforms such as Facebook.[2] This development is especially supported by the harmful effects hate speech has on its recipients [15].

Based on the research that identifies a difference in language and topic in conversations between adolescents and adults [16], it is necessary to build a database of youth language to explore the impact the language has upon algorithmic hate speech detection. This research lays the groundwork to close the gap by introducing an annotated hate speech data set focusing on youth language. The data set was collected in a real-world environment between March 2021 and June 2022. It provides the scientific community a modern corpus that can be used to evaluate the bias in existing classification algorithms for hate speech and further train domain specific algorithms to the setting of hate speech within the online chat conversations of adolescents. This modern real-world data set overcomes the status quo of identifying hate speech connected to geolocation and introduces the view that hate speech is also unique to international group conversations on the internet. It provides the field not just an age annotated data set, but introduces data collected from the chat platform discord in connection with an unseen real-world

---

[1] Forbes Media, accessed on 23.03.2023, https://www.forbes.com/sites/niallmccarthy/2020/05/13/facebook-removes-record-number-of-hate-speech-posts-infographic/?sh=20c0ef983035.

[2] Meta AI, accessed on 23.03.2023, https://ai.facebook.com/blog/how-facebook-uses-super-efficient-ai-models-to-detect-hate-speech.

J. Fillies (✉) · A. Paschke
Institut für Angewandte Informatik, Goerdelerring 9, 04109 Leipzig, Germany
e-mail: fillies@infai.org

Freie Universität Berlin, Kaiserswerther Str. 16-18, 14195 Berlin, Germany

S. Peikert · A. Paschke
Fraunhofer-Institut für Offene Kommunikationssysteme FOKUS, Kaiserin-Augusta-Allee 31, 10589 Berlin, Germany

© The Author(s), under exclusive license to Springer Nature Switzerland AG 2024
P. Haber et al. (eds.), *Data Science—Analytics and Applications*,
https://doi.org/10.1007/978-3-031-42171-6_5

chat conversation spreading over a time period of 15 months. Contrary to similar data sets, this research does not focus on filtered Tweets or comments. It is available, on request, for further research at Zenodo.org.[3]

2   Related Literature

Annotated data sets in the field of hate speech detection are available (e.g. [7, 20]) though there are fewer multilingual data sets with fitting annotations available [4]. Hate speech data sets have many annotation schemes [4], from binary to multi-class hierarchies. Other universal annotation schemes exist [11] and are deployed in hate speech annotation or similar contexts, such as cyberbullying [17]. It is difficult to obtain hate speech data sets and hate speech information within adolescents. Research focusing on cyberbullying in pre-teens can be found in the research of Sprugnoli et al. [17]. They created a data set containing annotated hate speech chat conversations between Italian high school students. The data set was created in an experimental setting to foster a safe environment, moderated by the researcher. In 2019, Menini et al. [12] presented a monitoring system for cyberbullying. They identified a network of multiple high schools, their students and their friends in the United Kingdom's Instagram community. In 2020, Wijesiriwardene et al. [21] published a multimodal data set containing Tweets labeled for toxic social media interactions. The data set was created focusing on American high school students. In 2011, Bayzick [1] created a data set consisting of messages from MySpace.com. They organized the messages into groups of ten and annotated the messages, some of which contained cyberbullying. The data set includes self-provided information about the age of the author. Dadvar et al. [5] showed that user context, including attributes such as age, gender, and cyberbullying history of the user, improves the detection of cyberbullying. Chen et al. [3] analyzes the personal writing style and other user specific attributes to identify the potential of the user spreading hate speech. To give closer understanding of the mentioned data sets, the key attributes are displayed in Table 1.

Natural language processing is required to be algorithmically fair and fitted to many social groups [2]. Classification algorithms can be biased towards many minority groups of people, for example, bias by gender [10] or race [9]. Even though age is a known source for bias in data [8], it is not widely analyzed in pretrained networks. To counter these biases, there are different approaches. Some focus on single domains, or tasks, via fine-tuning using new data [14].

As shown, there are numerous publicly available hate speech data sets, some of which address the adolescent audience and are annotated for cyberbullying or hate speech. However, there are three missing fields. Firstly, our research focuses on online conversations, not comments under posts. Secondly, the introduced dataset is drawn out of a real-world setting and not created in an artificial experimental setting. Thirdly, this data focuses on an international online English-speaking community, not a regional community.

The aspect of time needs to be considered, as it is necessary to collect and analyze the data sets from a recent time frame, considering the shifts in topic and language.

Within the last five years, no real-world hate speech data set containing online conversations of adolescents could be found.

3   Hate Speech Data Set

3.1   Methodology

Vidgen and Derczynski [19] recommend addressing the following points when creating an abusive content data set: purpose, explore new source, clear taxonomy, develop guidelines iteratively with your annotators, and data statement.

In the context of this research, the points are addressed as follows:

- Purpose: the purpose of this data set is to build a base for validation and improve hate speech detection within youth language, further explained in Sect. 1 ("Introduction").
- Explore new source: no hate speech Discord data set has been discovered so far.
- Clear taxonomy: the used taxonomy is based on Paasch-Colberg et al. [13] and is described in the Sect. 3.3 ("Annotation Guidelines").
- Develop guidelines iteratively with your annotators: this has been done and is described in the Sect. 3.4 ("Annotations Procedure").
- Data Statement: a data statement is provided using the format suggested by Gebru et al. [6].

---

[3] Zenodo.org, accessed on 13.04.2023, https://doi.org/10.5281/zenodo.7824768.

Table 1 Table of the mentioned existing data sets and the new introduced data set

Title	Author	Topic	Timeframe	Language	Platform	Number of entries	Percentage of hate speech (%)	Number of participants	Age of authors available
Hate speech dataset from a white supremacy forum	Gibert et al. [7]	Hate speech	2002–2017	English	Stormfront	9.916	11,29	Unknown	No
Creating a whatsapp dataset to study pre-teen cyberbullying	Sprugnoli et al. [17]	Cyberbullying	2018 or earlier	Italian	WhatsApp	ca. 2927 (14.600 tokens)	41,1	70	Yes
Alone: A dataset for toxic behavior among adolescents on twitter	Wijesiriwardene et al. [21]	Toxic Behavior	up to May 2018	English	Twitter	688 Interactions	17,15	Unknown	No
Detecting the presence of cyberbullying using computer software	Bayzick et al. [1]	Cyberbullying	2011	English	Myspace	4.813	21,0	Unknown	Yes
Hateful Symbols or Hateful People? Predictive Features for Hate Speech Detection on Twitter	Waseem and Hovy [20]	Cyberbullying	before 2012	English	Youtube	4.626	9,7	3.858	Yes
Hateful Messages: A Conversational Data Set of Hate Speech produced by Adolescents on Discord	Removed for Review	Hate Speech	3.2021–06.2022	English	Discord	88.395	6,42	249	Yes

3.2 Data Identification

Discord is a chat platform that provides spaces for communication between users. These servers are publicly available and, if configured, could be joined by anybody interested. There are public lists available for existing chat servers, filterable by language, name, and topics. The research project pre-selected a list of servers based on their names and descriptions. The pre-selected servers were further evaluated following these five criteria: Firstly, conversation language in English. Secondly, high appearance of general derogatory terms through a simple key word search. Thirdly, amount of active users. Fourthly, amount of messages sent in the group chat. And lastly, available information on the age of the users. The chosen server fulfills these criteria and was exported for the purpose of furthering research within the topic.

3.3 Annotation Guidelines

The annotation guidelines were developed iteratively with and by the annotators, ensuring a high understanding of the process and definitions. A common definition of hate speech was established as follows: a statement is viewed as hate speech if it is directed towards a group or an individual of a group with the characteristic of excluding or stigmatizing. A statement is further considered hate speech if it is hostile or implies the desire to harm or incite violence. Based on Paasch-Colberg et al. [13] a new annotation schema was defined including descriptions and examples. All nine categories of the schema are explained in the following Table 2.

3.4 Annotations Procedure

Five annotators have annotated the data set. The team of annotators consisted of Bachelor and Master computer science students, and the average age of the members was 29 years. The ages varied from 21 to 58 years. The team consisted of two female and three male annotators. For four out of five members, the ethnic background and mother tongue was German. One

Table 2 Table of annotated classes

Label	Definition	Example
No Hate	Positive and neutral conversations, but also criticism, rejection and disliking	"I don't like the new chairs"
Negative Stereotyping	Generalizations in which hurtful intent is a central motivator	"All blondes are stupid"
Dehumanization	Non-human character traits are attributed to humans, people, or groups. They are paired with elements not belonging to the human species	"Asian rats"
Violence and Killing	Endorse, glorify, or fantasize about violence or killing, the explicit call to violence and murder	"The only thing that [...] helps is pure violence"
Equation	Associates' people and groups of people with negative characteristics	"Poor = Africa"
Norm. of Exi. Dis.	Existing discrimination is downplayed and or manifested	"No wonder blacks are treated this way."
Disguise as Irony	Disguises negative statements as irony and downplays them as humor	"In my next life I'll be a social welfare recipient, there I can chill"
Harmful Slander	All other forms of insults and hurtful statements that cannot be classified into the previous labels	"I don't know any "normal" Jew"
Skip	Comments that cannot be understood and not assigned to labels above, due to a linguistic or symbolic barrier	Examples of this are emojis or Asian characters

Table 3 The data statement

Characteristic	Description
CURATION RATIONALE	The data set consists of Discord chat massages. The chat room was selected due to the high level of hate speech, the age of the authors and the platform's young user base
LANGUAGE VARIETY	The messages are online, written in English, and provided by a multinational setting, predominantly Europe, United Kingdom and America. It is partly youth language
SPEAKER DEMOGRAPHIC	There are 249 unique author IDs. In the data set and, the average age of the user who provided information was under 20. Out of the users who provided information, 19 are female and 22 male. Out of the users who provided information, 15 were from the UK, 18 from the USA, 17 from Europe, and 13 from other countries. Disordered speech is present
ANNOTATOR DEMOGRAPHIC	Five annotators were used. They are full time students with an age range between 21–58, average age 29. The group consisted of three males, two females, four native German speakers, one native Albanian speaker. Four members were German natives and one member was an native Albanian. Lastly, one member holds a degree as a translator
SPEECH SITUATION	The data set was collected between 26.03.21 and 15.06.2022. It consists of written unscripted asynchronous messages. And the intended audience were the other participants in the chat
TEXT CHARACTERISTICS	It is an everyday conversational setting which guarantees its members free speech

annotator's mother tongue and ethnic background was Albanian. One group member brought domain-specific knowledge through a degree as a translator.

The data set was divided into equal parts so that simultaneous annotation was possible. An annotation tool was used. Messages that were uncertain or not clear for the annotator were jointly annotated in the peer review process.

3.5   Data Statement

The statement is provided in Table 3 and based on Gebru et al. [6]. The classes "RECORDING QUALITY", "OTHER", and "PROVENANCE APPENDIX" were not available or applicable for the data set.

4   Data Evaluation

The evaluation is oriented on the data evaluation performed by de Gibert et al. [7]. The hate speech data set contains online conversations of adolescents on Discord, written in English. All messages have time stamps and author id's attached. The users are from different countries, mainly the USA, the EU, and GB. The data set consists of 88.395 messages. Out of these, 35.553 have an age annotation available and 52.895 do not. Table 4 shows the distribution of messages over all nine annotated categories. It is visible that the classes are not balanced, with most classes having less than 1.000 messages assigned and the non hate speech class dominates with over 87% of the data set. The whole data set contains 6,41% hateful messages and the age annotated subset contains 5,07% hateful messages. There are 9 members in the age group 14–17, 19 members in the age group 18–25, and 4 members in the age group 26+.

The distribution of the comments in relation to the 249 registered users shows directly that 90% of all messages were written by 30 users. On average, a user posts 2662 messages to the chat room, and 90% of the hate speech was produced by 85 users with an average user posting 60 hateful messages. It was discovered that one highly active user wrote 33.372 messages, accounting for 2488 or 43,87% of the hateful messages. This user is not classified as a chatbot and did not provide data regarding their age, therefore is not influencing the age annotated data sub set. In the age annotated sub set, 90% of the messages are attributed to 10 users, with 35 users providing 90% of the hateful messages in the sub set, sending an average of 54 hateful messages per user.

Based on de Gibert et al. [7] a hate score (HS) for each word (w) has been calculated as a simple way to create insight into the context in which a word appears. For this, all hateful classes (hate) have been combined into one. A Pointwise Mutual Information (PMI) score has been calculated between each word, the hateful class, and the non-hateful (nohate) class. The PMI score considers the relationship between the joint probability (P) and the product of the individual probabilities of two instances. Based on this, the hate score of each word was calculated by subtracting the non-hateful PMI from the hateful PMI.

Table 4 Table with distribution of labels

Label	All messages	Percentage of all messages	Messages with age attributes	Percentage of messages with age attributes
No Hate	77.034	87,15	31.037	87,30
Negative Stereotyping	768	0,9	232	0,7
Dehumanization	499	0,6	165	0,5
Violence and Killing	651	0,7	205	0,6
Equation	124	0,1	27	0,08
Norm. of Exi. Dis.	145	0,2	40	0,1
Disguise as Irony	181	0,2	60	0,2
Harmful Slander	3.303	3,7	1.075	3,0
Skip	5.689	6,4	2.712	7,6
Total	88.395	100	35.553	100

Table 5 Table with the most positive (hateful) and most negative (least hateful) HS

Hateful terms	Hate score	Non-hateful terms	Hate score
ni**er	11,0493	👀	−4.4188
b*tch	9,6315	fair	−4.0526
fa*got	9,2531	🛸	−3.6197
h*e	9,1535	plus	−3.4836
kys	7,4165	huh	−3.4132

$$PMI(w, hate) = log_2 \frac{P(w, hate)}{P(w)P(hate)} \tag{1}$$

$$HS(w) = PMI(w, hate) - PMI(w, nohate) \tag{2}$$

The Table 5 displays the five words with the highest and lowest correlation to the hateful class. The hateful terms were modified to reduce their impact on the reader. The hateful words are strong, well known slurs and defamations. The least correlated term is an emoticon followed by general words including the word "fair". In these ten words, a youthful character can be identified, for example, by the extensive emoticon use and the usage of hateful modern abbreviation such as "kys". Overall, there are 3542 words with a negative Hate Score and 1608 words with a positive Hate Score.

5   Discussion

It is important to understand that online chat rooms, like the one evaluated, are an ecosystem, meaning the users influence each other in language and topic. Therefore, this youth language corpus might be fundamentally different from other youth language corpora. The approach used in this paper is an important contribution to the world of youth language data sets due to the use of modern language with the provided self-identification, putting the general discussion in an age range under 20.

There is no way to guarantee that the given age ranges are truthful. This limitation cannot be easily circumvented in a non-experimental setting if a real-world data set guaranteeing data protection is wanted.

During the creation of the data set, which followed the official recommendation, the classes of the annotation schema were developed in communication with the annotators. This arguably led to an improvable annotation schema. Similarly, it is arguable that the used form of communal decision on uncertain classifications is not transparent and missing inter-annotator agreements. The work is open to updates and changes in the class definitions or reannotation.

The data set is heavily unbalanced in regard to authorship of the messages and the labeled hate speech classes. Furthermore, it is clear that the number of authors in general is small. These factors are due to the real-life character of the data set and are common problems in the field of hate speech.

It is important to start collecting and publishing subdomain data sets to understand the difference and uniqueness of languages in these groups and to best identify performing hate speech classification algorithms.

6   Conclusion and Future Work

This paper collected and annotated a youth language data set containing 88.395 online chat messages. It provides an unseen amount of unfiltered annotated conversational data between multiple international authors, novel to the domain of hate speech detection.

Of the 249 unique users, 31 provided information about their age, averaging to under 20 years. The data set is labeled into nine classes in the field of hate speech. A data analysis has been conducted and influential terms for the "Hate" and "No Hate" classes have been established. A data statement is provided. The data set is available for scientific research.

This research is the ground for further work in the field of hate speech detection within youth language. The next step is to identify a non youth language online chat conversation and annotate it for hate speech, comparing the differences in language and use of hateful terms. Overall, the research can be used to train youth language specific hate speech classifiers and identify the influence of youth language on their performance.

This research opens up the possibility to analyze the bias youth language introduces into existing pretrained hate speech detection models. Furthermore, the generalizability of existing prediction models can be tested and increased by using this new data set. Lastly, topics of interest within groups of adolescent can be established and compared to other communities or research results.

Acknowledgements This research was supported by the Citizens, Equality, Rights and Values (CERV) Programme under Grand Agreement No. 101049342.

References

1. Bayzick, J., Kontostathis, A., Edwards, L.: Detecting the presence of cyberbullying using computer software (2011)
2. Blodgett, S.L., O'Connor, B.: Racial Disparity in Natural Language Processing: A Case Study of Social Media African-American English. arXiv e-prints arXiv:1707.00061 (Jun 2017). https://doi.org/10.48550/arXiv.1707.00061
3. Chen, Y., Zhou, Y., Zhu, S., Xu, H.: Detecting offensive language in social media to protect adolescent online safety. In: 2012 International Conference on Privacy, Security, Risk and Trust and 2012 International Conference on Social Computing, pp. 71–80 (2012). https://doi.org/10.1109/SocialCom-PASSAT.2012.55
4. Chung, Y.L., Kuzmenko, E., Tekiroglu, S.S., Guerini, M.: CONAN – COunter NArratives through nichesourcing: a multilingual dataset of responses to fight online hate speech. In: Proceedings of the 57th Annual Meeting of the Association for Computational Linguistics, pp. 2819–2829. Association for Computational Linguistics, Florence, Italy (Jul 2019). https://doi.org/10.18653/v1/P19-1271, https://aclanthology.org/P19-1271
5. Dadvar, M., Trieschnigg, D., Ordelman, R., de Jong, F.: Improving cyberbullying detection with user context, pp. 693–696 (1 2013). https://doi.org/10.1007/978-3-642-36973-5_62
6. Gebru, T., Morgenstern, J., Vecchione, B., Vaughan, J.W., Wallach, H., III, H.D., Crawford, K.: Datasheets for datasets. Commun. ACM **64**(12), 86–92 (2021). https://doi.org/10.1145/3458723, https://doi.org/10.1145/3458723
7. de Gibert, O., Perez, N., García-Pablos, A., Cuadros, M.: Hate speech dataset from a white supremacy forum. In: Proceedings of the 2nd Workshop on Abusive Language Online (ALW2), pp. 11–20. Association for Computational Linguistics, Brussels, Belgium (Oct 2018). https://doi.org/10.18653/v1/W18-5102, https://aclanthology.org/W18-5102
8. Hovy, D., Prabhumoye, S.: Five sources of bias in natural language processing. Lang. Linguist. Compass **15**(8), e12432 (2021). https://doi.org/10.1111/lnc3.12432, https://compass.onlinelibrary.wiley.com/doi/abs/10.1111/lnc3.12432
9. Kennedy, B., Jin, X., Mostafazadeh Davani, A., Dehghani, M., Ren, X.: Contextualizing hate speech classifiers with post-hoc explanation. In: Proceedings of the 58th Annual Meeting of the Association for Computational Linguistics, pp. 5435–5442. Association for Computational Linguistics, Online (Jul 2020). https://doi.org/10.18653/v1/2020.acl-main.483, https://aclanthology.org/2020.acl-main.483
10. Kurita, K., Vyas, N., Pareek, A., Black, A.W., Tsvetkov, Y.: Measuring bias in contextualized word representations. In: Proceedings of the First Workshop on Gender Bias in Natural Language Processing, pp. 166–172. Association for Computational Linguistics, Florence, Italy (Aug 2019). https://doi.org/10.18653/v1/W19-3823, https://aclanthology.org/W19-3823
11. Lenzi, V.B., Moretti, G., Sprugnoli, R.: Cat: the celct annotation tool. In: Chair, N.C.C., Choukri, K., Declerck, T., Doğan, M.U., Maegaard, B., Mariani, J., Moreno, A., Odijk, J., Piperidis, S. (eds.) Proceedings of the Eight International Conference on Language Resources and Evaluation (LREC'12). European Language Resources Association (ELRA), Istanbul, Turkey (May 2012)
12. Menini, S., Moretti, G., Corazza, M., Cabrio, E., Tonelli, S., Villata, S.: A system to monitor cyberbullying based on message classification and social network analysis. In: Proceedings of the Third Workshop on Abusive Language Online, pp. 105–110. Association for Computational Linguistics, Florence, Italy (Aug 2019). https://doi.org/10.18653/v1/W19-3511, https://aclanthology.org/W19-3511
13. Paasch-Colberg, S., Strippel, C., Trebbe, J., Emmer, M.: From insult to hate speech: mapping offensive language in German user comments on immigration. Media Commun. **9**(1), 171–180 (2021). https://doi.org/10.17645/mac.v9i1.3399

14. Park, J.H., Shin, J., Fung, P.: Reducing gender bias in abusive language detection. In: Proceedings of the 2018 Conference on Empirical Methods in Natural Language Processing, pp. 2799–2804. Association for Computational Linguistics, Brussels, Belgium (Oct–Nov 2018). https://doi.org/10.18653/v1/D18-1302

15. Saha, K., Chandrasekharan, E., De Choudhury, M.: Prevalence and psychological effects of hateful speech in online college communities. In: Proceedings of the 10th ACM Conference on Web Science, pp. 255–264. WebSci '19, Association for Computing Machinery, New York, NY, USA (2019). https://doi.org/10.1145/3292522.3326032

16. Schwartz, H.A., Eichstaedt, J.C., Kern, M.L., Dziurzynski, L., Ramones, S.M., Agrawal, M., Shah, A., Kosinski, M., Stillwell, D., Seligman, M.E.P., Ungar, L.H.: Personality, gender, and age in the language of social media: the open-vocabulary approach. PLOS ONE 8(9), 1–16 (09 2013). https://doi.org/10.1371/journal.pone.0073791

17. Sprugnoli, R., Menini, S., Tonelli, S., Oncini, F., Piras, E.: Creating a WhatsApp dataset to study pre-teen cyberbullying. In: Proceedings of the 2nd Workshop on Abusive Language Online (ALW2), pp. 51–59. Association for Computational Linguistics, Brussels, Belgium (Oct 2018). https://doi.org/10.18653/v1/W18-5107, https://aclanthology.org/W18-5107

18. Thapa, R., Subedi, S.: Social media and depression. J. Psychiatr. Assoc. Nepal 7(2), 1–4 (2018). https://doi.org/10.3126/jpan.v7i2.24607, https://www.nepjol.info/index.php/JPAN/article/view/24607

19. Vidgen, B., Derczynski, L.: Directions in abusive language training data, a systematic review: Garbage in, garbage out. PLOS ONE 15(12), 1–32 (12 2021). https://doi.org/10.1371/journal.pone.0243300

20. Waseem, Z., Hovy, D.: Hateful symbols or hateful people? predictive features for hate speech detection on Twitter. In: Proceedings of the NAACL Student Research Workshop, pp. 88–93. Association for Computational Linguistics, San Diego, California (Jun 2016). https://doi.org/10.18653/v1/N16-2013, https://aclanthology.org/N16-2013

21. Wijesiriwardene, T., Inan, H., Kursuncu, U., Gaur, M., Shalin, V.L., Thirunarayan, K., Sheth, A., Arpinar, I.B.: Alone: a dataset for toxic behavior among adolescents on twitter. In: Social Informatics: 12th International Conference, SocInfo 2020, Pisa, Italy, Oct 6–9, 2020, Proceedings, pp. 427–439. Springer, Berlin, Heidelberg (2020). https://doi.org/10.1007/978-3-030-60975-7_31

Prediction of Tourism Flow with Sparse Geolocation Data

Julian Lemmel, Zahra Babaiee, Marvin Kleinlehner, Ivan Majic, Philipp Neubauer, Johannes Scholz, Radu Grosu, and Sophie Neubauer

Abstract Modern tourism in the 21st century is facing numerous challenges. Among these the rapidly growing number of tourists visiting space-limited regions like historical cities, museums and bottlenecks such as bridges is one of the biggest. In this context, a proper and accurate prediction of tourism volume and tourism flow within a certain area is important and critical for visitor management tasks such as sustainable treatment of the environment and prevention of overcrowding. Static flow control methods like conventional low-level controllers or limiting access to overcrowded venues could not solve the problem yet. In this paper, we empirically evaluate the performance of state-of-the-art deep-learning methods such as RNNs, GNNs, and Transformers as well as the classic statistical ARIMA method. Granular limited data supplied by a tourism region is extended by exogenous data such as geolocation trajectories of individual tourists, weather and holidays. In the field of visitor flow prediction with sparse data, we are thereby capable of increasing the accuracy of our predictions, incorporating modern input feature handling as well as mapping geolocation data on top of discrete POI data.

Keywords Tourism · Time series forecasting · Sustainable tourism · Sparse geolocation data

1   Introduction

With increasing population and travel capacities (e.g. easy access to international flights) cultural tourism destinations have seen a rise in visitors. In addition, recent needs for social distancing and attendance limitations due to the global COVID-19 pandemic have confronted tourism destinations with significant challenges in e.g. creating and establishing sustainable treatment of the both urbanised and natural environment or e.g. preventing overcrowded waiting-lines. The perception of tourists regarding health hazards, safety and unpleasant tourism experiences may be influenced by social distance and better physical separation [21].

Based on The United Nation's 2030 Agenda for Sustainable Development [22], tourism is obligated to contribute to several Sustainable Development Goals, including sustainable cities, responsible consumption, and economic growth. Sustainable tourism can achieve this by understanding and controlling visitor flows, preserving natural landmarks, reducing emissions and waste, establishing sustainable energy consumption, creating harmony between residents and tourists, and maximizing tourist satisfaction for economic prosperity.

Insufficient data availability in real-world problems is caused by factors such as compliance issues, lack of data collection, and transfer. Nonpersonal data from POIs, tourist facilities, and anonymized digital device data are used in research, but

Julian Lemmel and Zahra Babaiee—Equal Contribution.

J. Lemmel (✉) · Z. Babaiee · M. Kleinlehner · P. Neubauer · S. Neubauer
Datenvorsprung GmbH, Vienna, Austria
e-mail: julian.lemmel@tuwien.ac.at

J. Lemmel · Z. Babaiee · R. Grosu · S. Neubauer
CPS Group, Technische Universität Wien, Vienna, Austria

I. Majic · J. Scholz
Technische Universität Graz, Graz, Austria

© The Author(s), under exclusive license to Springer Nature Switzerland AG 2024
P. Haber et al. (eds.), *Data Science—Analytics and Applications*,
https://doi.org/10.1007/978-3-031-42171-6_6

location data collected by mobile apps is controversial due to profit-oriented collection practices. It's important to consider whether people are aware of what they're sharing when using these services, even if the datasets don't contain direct personal data.

The question of how to improve awareness of data shared by such apps or services is not answered in this research. This scientific work is focusing on what is possible to achieve in the given environment considering the given data and data history in regards to tourist flow prediction since sparse data is a widespread generic problem.

The first step in order to control tourist flows is to predict authentic movement and behavior patterns. However, since the tourist visitor flow is affected by many factors such as the weather, cultural events, holidays, and regional traffic and hotspots throughout a specific day, it is a very challenging task to accurately predict the future flow [13]. Due to the availability of large datasets and computational resources, deep neural networks became the state-of-the-art methods in the task of forecasting time-series data [18], including tourism flow applications [19].

In this work, we focus on tourist flow prediction based on a local dataset from the visitors of the tourist attractions of the city of Salzburg as well as third-party geolocation data of individual tourists. After data preprocessing and dataset preparation, we attempt to compare the performance of different deep-learning-based methods for time-series prediction with ARIMA, a traditional statistics-based method. According to Li and Cao [12], ARIMA is the most popular classical time forecasting method based on exponential smoothing and it was made popular in the 1970s when it was proposed by Ahmed and Cook [1] to be used for short-term freeway traffic predictions.

We summarize the specific contributions of our paper as follows:

- We perform a comprehensive comparison of DL and ARIMA, a traditional technique, on a real-world dataset to reveal the shortcomings and point out necessary future improvements.
- Per point-of-interest (POI), we perform granular predictions on an hourly basis, which is critical for the task of tourism flow control.
- We further evaluate modern DL techniques such as Transformers and GNNs.
- To the best of our knowledge, we are the first to apply a wide range of DL models to tourist flow prediction.

2   Related Work

Considering the importance of predicting tourist flows in a growing industry, visitor forecasting has gained attention in recent years. Recurrent Neural Networks are used to forecast tourist demand, such as LSTMs that can be used in conjunction with deep neural networks or hidden Markov Models [12, 20]. Only a limited set of models is used in most of these studies to make predictions.

Another important aspect of tourism data is its granularity. Several studies focus on long-term estimates of monthly, quarterly, and yearly, or in the best case daily numbers of tourists in large regions as a measure of city or country-level tourism demand [2]. For tourism flow control, it is vital to perform granular predictions on an hourly basis and per POI.

DL-based models. Time-series data prediction is typically handled by recurrent neural networks (RNNs). With RNNs, neural networks gain memory, allowing them to forecast sequence-based data. Gated RNNs are able to produce a good performance as LSTM [9] and GRU [5].

The RNN has limitations when faced with irregularly sampled time series, such as that encountered in tourist flow forecasting. In order to overcome this limitation, phased-LSTM [16] adds a time gate to the LSTM cells. GRU-D [4] incorporates time intervals via a trainable decaying mechanism to deal with missing data and long-term dependence in time series.

Instead of discrete-time models, continuous-time models with latent state defined at all times can also be used, such as CT-RNN [7], CT-LSTM [14], and CT-GRU [15], as well as NeuralODEs [6], which define the hidden state of the network as a solution to an ordinary differential equation. Augmented-NeuralODEs [6] can alleviate some limitations of NeuralODEs, such as non-intersecting trajectories, by using augmentation strategies. These continuous-time models have favorable properties, such as adaptive computation and training with constant memory cost. GoTube [8] can be used to statistically verify them by constructing stochastic reach tubes of continuous-time systems.

On the other hand, transformer-based models [23] have been successful in various applications due to their powerful capability for sequence learning and representation. They have also been explored in time-series forecasting tasks for datasets with long sequences and high historical information. The multi-head self-attention mechanism is the primary component of transformer models, which can extract correlations in long sequences. However, the permutation-invariant nature of self-attention requires positional encodings to prevent the loss of temporal dependencies.

Graph Neural Networks (GNNs) are an interesting new class of Deep Learning Algorithms that allow for the inputs to be structured as graphs. Most GNN models build on the notion of Graph Convolutions which can be seen as a generalization of Convolutional Neural Networks to graph structured data—as opposed to being arranged in a grid. An even more fascinating type of DL models are temporal GNNs that combine Graph Convolutions with RNNs. Such temporal GNN models are most prominent in traffic flow prediction applications [26].

Traditional techniques. For time-series forecasting with traditional techniques we use the Autoregressive Integrated Moving Average (ARIMA) model. ARIMA has been used in recent studies as a baseline for the evaluation of novel deep-learning based models [25] and is thus selected as a baseline model for this paper as well.

3 Data

Two different data sources were combined to enable the use of their different features in the training of the models and prediction of future visitor counts.

The first dataset we used stems from the "Salzburg Card" which was kindly provided to us by TSG Tourismus Salzburg GmbH. Upon purchase of these cards, the owner has the ability to enter 32 different tourist attractions and museums included in the portfolio of the Salzburg Card. The dataset consists of the time-stamps of entries to each POI. Additionally, we used data about weather and holidays in Austria.

We utilized mobile phone location data from a third-party service to improve tourist flow predictions in Salzburg. The dataset covers around 3% of tourists and provides information on the number of tourists between points of interest. However, the data is sparse and lacks a distinct recording frequency. To further improve our predictions, we incorporated a street graph obtained from OpenStreetMap [17] using the `osmnx` python package. The resulting graph contains 2064 nodes and 5359 edges, with edge values corresponding to the lengths of the street segments. We then mapped the location data to the graph by assigning each location to the nearest node and aggregating the total number per hour.

CoVID-19 Tourism around the globe saw huge drops during the global CoVID-19 pandemic. Starting in march of 2020, Austria started to take preemptive measures to prevent the spread of the virus. These travel restrictions and closings of public spaces, hotels and restaurants severely reduced the number of tourists in and around the city of Salzburg. As a consequence, prediction accuracy could be diminished when using models that have been trained on pre-CoVID data.

4 Methods

For this work, we built our own dataset on hourly data collected from tourist attractions and then expanded this by including geolocation data. Including many different datasources is a key challenge for this real-world prediction task. Sparse geolocation data is therefore fed into our GNN model as features. With this approach we aim to create models that are capable of easily integrating new datasources that might be available in the future. We then perform predictions with a rich set of models and do a comprehensive comparison of the results. In this section we first introduce the dataset we used for the experiments. Then we go over the methods we chose to evaluate and compare their performances.

4.1 Deep-Learning Models

We use a large set of RNN variations on the tourist-flow dataset to perform a comprehensive comparison of the state-of-the art models and provide insight on their performance. The set comprises vanilla-RNN, LSTM, phased-LSTM, GRU-D, CT-RNN, CT-LSTM and Neural-ODE networks. Moreover, we used a Transformer model, using only the encoder part with 8 heads, 64 hidden units, and 3 layers, to forecast the tourist flow. Finally, we applied a naive continuous-time temporal GNN approach based on CT-RNNs to our prediction problem in order to utilize geolocation data of individual tourists. All of the Neural

Networks were trained with Backpropagation-Through-Time and the Adam optimizer [11] using the parameters given in the appendix Table 3.

In order to incorporate inductive bias stemming from the street layout from Salzburg, we used a simplified CT-RNN based GNN model that we will call Continuous-Time Recurrent Graph Network (**CT-GRN**) in the following. It consists of one neuron per node in the street graph and exhibits the same connectivity. This is done by point-wise multiplying the recurrent kernel with the graph's normalized adjacency matrix whose entries are the inverse of the corresponding street segment lengths.

$$y_{t+1} = y_t - \tau y_t + a \odot \tanh((W_{rec} \odot \hat{A})y_t + W_{in}x_t + b)$$

where y_t is the network's state at time t, x_t is the exogenous input, τ, a, W_{rec}, W_{in} and b are trainable parameters, and $\hat{A} = D^{-1}A$ is the normalized Adjacency matrix. The resulting model inherits all the favourable ODE properties of CT-RNNs such as the ability to evaluate at arbitrary points in (continuous) time and differentiable dynamics used in verification. Finally, we used a variation of the *Teacher Forcing* [24] technique which basically translates to resetting the nodes of the network to the target value after each step. Our **Mixed Teacher Forcing** version forces the hidden state of the POI nodes to the true value and adds up the predicted and true values for the other nodes.

4.2   Traditional Methods

In this study, we used a non-seasonal ARIMA model (*ARIMA (p, d, q)*) that ignores seasonal patterns in a time-series, where p is the number of autoregressive terms, d is the number of non-seasonal differences, and q is the number of lagged forecast errors in the prediction equation [3]. We utilized the *auto.arima* function from the *R forecast* [10] library to automatically determine the best values for p, d, and q for each of the 32 POIs. The ARIMA model was then individually fitted to each POI's training dataset using the *pmdarima* library in Python. Each time the number of visitors is predicted for the next hour in the test data, the true value (i.e., number of visitors) for that hour is added to update the existing ARIMA model and make it aware of all previous values before making the next prediction. This approach prioritized prediction accuracy over time complexity.

4.3   Preprocessing

We used the Salzburg card data from years 2017, 2018, and 2019 for our first set of experiments. In order to create the time-series data, we accumulated the hourly entries to each location. The data then consists of the hour of the day, and the number of entries at that hour to each of the 32 POIs.

For the DL models, we added additional features to the dataset: Year, Month, Day of month, Day of week, Holidays and Weather data. For the Holiday data we used the national holidays and school holidays and count the days to the next school day. For the Weather data, we used the hourly weather data with these features: Temperature, Feels Like, Wind speed, Precipitation, and Clouds as well as a One-Hot-Encoded single word description of the weather (e.g. "Snow").

We performed further pre-processing by normalizing all features to values between 0 and 1. To account for seasons, we performed sine-cosine transformation for the month. Intuitively, since it is a circular feature we do not want to have the values for December and January to be far apart.

Finally, we split the data into sequences of length 30, and used the data from years 2017 and 2018 as the training set, and 2019 as the test set.

Graph Neural Networks For the GNN we used the OSM graphs as illustrated in Sect. 3. Our dataset of tourist locations was very sparse which subsequently resulted in very sparse inputs for each node. Since we are trying to predict numbers of entries at the POIs, we added them as additional nodes to the graph connecting them to up to 5 of the nearest nodes present in the graph with a max distance of 80 m. Finally, the global features such as weather and holidays are added to the graph by a linear mapping from features to nodes. This way we obtained a series of graphs where each sample constitutes the OSM graph with the edge values corresponding to the distance and the node values corresponding to the aggregated number of people near this location/POI entries. One sample is visualized in Fig. 1. For inference we predicted the whole graph and discarded the nodes that do not represent POIs.

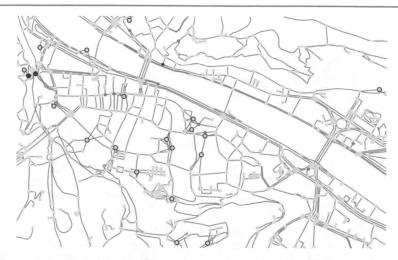

Fig. 1 One sample of the series of OSM graphs of the Salzburg city center obtained from preprocessing. Encircled nodes are the special POI nodes. Color coded are the normalized aggregated entry and tracking data, where most of the nodes indicate zero (pale)

5   Main Results

5.1   Forecasting Visitor Numbers

We performed a diverse set of experiments with ARIMA and DL models to evaluate their forecasting accuracy, execution time and prediction time and compare the models. Table 1 shows the Mean-Absolute-Error (MAE) and Root-Mean-Squared-Error (RMSE) achieved for each method applied to the timeframe from 2017–2019—before COVID. In order to find optimal model size, loss function, and whether to use normalized visitor counts, we did a grid search conducting three runs per configuration and keeping the one which achieved the lowest average RMSE. As a baseline we include the naive approach of using the last true value as prediction at each step, i.e. $\hat{y}_t = y_{t-1}$.

The table includes the model size, number of parameters, and training and prediction times for the best run of each deep-learning model. We excluded non-normalized models since normalized visitor counts consistently led to better results. MAE was the best loss function for all models except ANODE, which performed better with Huber loss. The phased LSTM achieved comparable results with the fewest parameters.

Our DL models outperformed ARIMA in both metrics, with and without additional features. Adding more features did not significantly improve performance, suggesting that it may lead to over-fitting. We report results with and without additional features for DL models to ensure fairness in comparison with ARIMA, which cannot use external features. Additionally, ARIMA struggles with short sequences, while DL models can handle them when trained on the full dataset.

Table 1 Averaged prediction errors

Model	# Cells/ # Parameters	Time Train (min)	Pred (ms)	Only visitors MAE	RMSE	External features MAE	RMSE
ARIMA	**224**	–	69k	5.217	7.833	–	–
ANODE	64/21.3k	145.6	3.01	4.599	6.965	4.410	6.663
Vanilla RNN	128/43.7k	5.9	**0.18**	3.958	6.321	3.802	6.160
LSTM	32/11.9k	**1.5**	0.24	3.713	6.209	3.630	6.113
Phased LSTM	32/**11.8k**	27.0	0.46	3.825	6.359	3.651	6.120
CT-LSTM	32/19.9k	18.1	0.31	3.734	6.239	3.700	6.185
CT-RNN	128/27.4k	57.1	0.60	3.694	6.131	3.629	**5.983**
GRU-D	64/27.7k	16.6	0.33	**3.638**	**6.121**	**3.621**	6.073
Naive	–	–	–	6.466	9.483	–	–

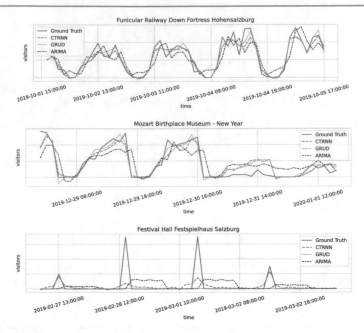

Fig. 2 Predicted and True visitor counts for the Funicular Railway (top) and Mozart's Birthplace Museum (mid) and the Festival Hall (bottom). Predictions are computed using CT-RNN (orange), GRU-D (green) and ARIMA (red)

In Table 1, we compare the training and prediction times of ARIMA and DL models. ARIMA took 69s to perform a single prediction for all POIs, while the DL models took fractions of milliseconds, with the trade-off of having longer training times. ARIMA does not have a dedicated training step, and its calculations are time-consuming since it makes predictions for each POI separately. In contrast, DL models are trained with the visitors to all POIs in a single vector and make predictions for all at the same time. This allows DL models to leverage implicit data about the total number of visitors in the city, which ARIMA loses.

In order to visually explore the predictions made by the models, we plotted the predictions and the ground truth for a few selected time-windows (see Fig. 2). We plot the predictions made by the DL models (including the external features) with the best MAE and RMSE, which were the GRU-D and CT-RNN respectively. The prediction made by the DL models with the visitors only data was only slightly worse than the others, which is why we omit these evaluations in the plots. Our plots show that although ARIMA is out-performed by the DL methods in the average error of all predictions, there are cases where it actually performs better than the other models. The plot on the Top shows the forecast and real values for the tourists entered the Funicular Railway descend which is the cable car ride leading up to Salzburg Castle. As visible in the plot, the DL models show a better performance, especially in the valleys where the ARIMA fails to predict the downfalls accurately. Mid shows visitor predictions for Mozart's Birthplace Museum around the time of New Year's Eve. The reduced numbers of visitors on the 1st and 2nd of January is overestimated by all our models. Finally, on the bottom the predictions for the Festival Hall Festspielhaus guided tour are shown which is sparse since it takes place once a day at 2 pm. All models fail in prediction for the second and third peak at this location. However, CT-RNN shows a very good performance in predicting the first and last peak and at least shows an upward trend for the second and third peak. ARIMA can not handle this type of sparse data at all.

5.2   Including Geolocation Data

We conducted a second set of experiments on the timeframe from 2019 to 2021 that includes geolocation data of individual (anonymized) tourists. Results are presented in Table 2 which shows for each model the number of Parameters and MAE with and without additional features and also when using features and the geolocation data. This time we included the Transformer and GNN models, but excluded ARIMA due to computation time reasons. Since the *Salzburg Card dataset* for this particular timeframe contains a significantly lower number of datapoints due to lockdowns enforced by the government, the numbers must not be compared directly to the results discussed in the last section.

Table 2 Average prediction results for 2021 after training on data from 2019 and 2020

Model	MAE		
	only visitors	+ features	+ geolocation
Vanilla RNN	2.48	2.42	3.37
LSTM	2.66	2.58	3.54
Phased LSTM	2.44	2.44	3.05
CT-LSTM	2.61	2.57	3.32
CT-RNN	2.50	2.45	3.16
ANODE	2.63	2.57	3.64
GRU-D	2.99	2.87	3.58
Transformer	2.19	**2.04**	2.65
Naive	2.187	–	–
CT-GRN	–	–	**2.63**

This time the naive approach outlined above led to surprisingly good results and only the Transformers with exogenous features were able to surpass it. Transformers can handle multi-variate data well due to the multi-head self-attention mechanism which enables them to extract hidden correlations in input, and hence get better loss after using additional features. However, they require considerably more parameters in comparison to the RNN models.

For the GNN we only conducted experiments with additional geolocation data since input graph attributes would be even sparser without, defeating the point of using a graph based approach. The CT-GRN algorithm scored a slightly worse prediction error in comparison to the other models when not using visitors and features as input. However, all other methods scored worse when trained on the sparse geolocation data which shows the usefulness of the GNN approach.

Our GNN approach enables us to incorporate the sparse geolocation data into our model. Since there is more sparse geolocation data expected to be processed within real-life-scenarios, this is the only approach to fit these needs.

6 Conclusions and Future Work

Our study demonstrated the effectiveness of DL models for tourist flow time-series forecasting, particularly when external features are included. DL models outperformed the traditional ARIMA method and were faster in terms of prediction time. We also showed that GNNs are more suitable for incorporating spatial structure using sparse geolocation data.

Moving forward, there are several directions for future research. One possibility is to investigate methods to further improve the performance of DL models, such as implementing regularization or learning rate scheduling. Another option is to explore the use of Vector Auto-Regression (VAR) to address the limitations of ARIMA for univariate data. Finally, we plan to develop specialized models that can outperform existing state-of-the-art models in short-term prediction, with the ultimate goal of helping tourism stakeholders make informed decisions and promote sustainable tourism practices.

Acknowledgements This work is supported by the Austrian Research Promotion Agency (FFG) Project grant No. FO999887513. SG is partially funded by the Austrian Science Fund (FWF) project number W1255-N23. Map data copyrighted OpenStreetMap contributors and available from https://www.openstreetmap.org.

Appendix

Hyperparameters

See Table 3.

Table 3 Hyperparameters
used in RNN training

Hyperparameter	Value
Sequence length	30
Batch size	16
Epochs	300
Optimizer	adam
Learning-rate	$1e^{-3}$
$\beta_{1,2}$	$(0.9, 0.999)$
ϵ	$1e^{-8}$
Loss Function	mse, mae, huber
Model size	32, 64, 128
Normalized visitors	True, False

References

1. Ahmed, M.S., Cook, A.R.: Analysis of freeway traffic time-series data by using box-jenkins techniques. Transp. Res. Rec. (722) (1979). ISBN: 9780309029728
2. Asvikarani, A., Widiartha, I., Raharja, M.: Foreign tourist arrival forecasting to bali using cascade forward backpropagation. Jurnal Ilmiah Kursor **10**(4) (2020)
3. Burger, C.J.S.C., Dohnal, M., Kathrada, M., Law, R.: A practitioners guide to time-series methods for tourism demand forecasting — a case study of Durban, South Africa. Tour. Manag. **22**(4), 403–409 (2001)
4. Che, Z., Purushotham, S., Cho, K., Sontag, D., Liu, Y.: Recurrent neural networks for multivariate time series with missing values. Sci. Rep. **8**(1) (2018)
5. Chung, J., Gülçehre, Ç., Cho, K., Bengio, Y.: Empirical evaluation of gated recurrent neural networks on sequence modeling. CoRR **abs/1412.3555** (2014)
6. Dupont, E., Doucet, A., Teh, Y.W.: Augmented Neural ODEs. arXiv:1904.01681 [cs, stat] (Oct 2019)
7. Funahashi, K., Nakamura, Y.: Approximation of dynamical systems by continuous time recurrent neural networks. Neural Netw. **6**(6), 801–806 (1993)
8. Gruenbacher, S., Lechner, M., Hasani, R., Rus, D., Henzinger, T.A., Smolka, S.A., Grosu, R.: Gotube: scalable statistical verification of continuous-depth models. AAAI (May 2022)
9. Hochreiter, S., Schmidhuber, J.: Long short-term memory. Neural Comput. **9**(8), 1735–1780 (1997)
10. Hyndman, R.J., Khandakar, Y.: Automatic time series forecasting: the forecast package for R. J. Stat. Softw. **27**(3), 1–22 (2008)
11. Kingma, D.P., Ba, J.: Adam: a method for stochastic optimization (2014), cite arxiv:1412.6980Comment: Published as a Conference Paper at the 3rd International Conference for Learning Representations, San Diego (2015)
12. Li, Y., Cao, H.: Prediction for tourism flow based on LSTM neural network. Procedia Comput. Sci. **129**, 277–283 (2018)
13. Liu, L., Zhang, R., Peng, J., Li, G., Du, B., Lin, L.: Attentive crowd flow machines. CoRR **abs/1809.00101** (2018)
14. Mei, H., Eisner, J.M.: The neural hawkes process: a neurally self-modulating multivariate point process. In: Guyon, I., Luxburg, U.V., Bengio, S., Wallach, H., Fergus, R., Vishwanathan, S., Garnett, R. (eds.) Advances in Neural Information Processing Systems, vol. 30. Curran Associates, Inc. (2017)
15. Mozer, M.C., Kazakov, D., Lindsey, R.V.: Discrete event, continuous time RNNs. CoRR **abs/1710.04110** (2017)
16. Neil, D., Pfeiffer, M., Liu, S.C.: Phased lstm: Accelerating recurrent network training for long or event-based sequences. In: Lee, D., Sugiyama, M., Luxburg, U., Guyon, I., Garnett, R. (eds.) Advances in Neural Information Processing Systems, vol. 29. Curran Associates, Inc. (2016)
17. OpenStreetMap contributors: Planet dump retrieved from https://planet.osm.org. https://www.openstreetmap.org (2017)
18. Pan, Q., Hu, W., Chen, N.: Two birds with one stone: series saliency for accurate and interpretable multivariate time series forecasting. In: Zhou, Z.H. (ed.) Proceedings of the Thirtieth International Joint Conference on Artificial Intelligence, IJCAI-21, pp. 2884–2891. International Joint Conferences on Artificial Intelligence Organization (8 2021), main Track
19. Prilistya, S.K., Erna Permanasari, A., Fauziati, S.: Tourism demand time series forecasting: a systematic literature review. In: 2020 12th International Conference on Information Technology and Electrical Engineering (ICITEE), pp. 156–161 (2020)
20. Rizal, A.A., Hartati, S.: Recurrent neural network with extended Kalman filter for prediction of the number of tourist arrival in Lombok. In: 2016 International Conference on Informatics and Computing (ICIC), pp. 180–185 (2016)
21. Sigala, M.: Tourism and covid-19: impacts and implications for advancing and resetting industry and research. J. Bus. Res. **117**, 312–321 (2020)
22. UNWTO, U.N.W.T.O.: Tourism in the 2030 Agenda. https://www.unwto.org/tourism-in-2030-agenda (2015), [Online; accessed 20-September-2022]
23. Vaswani, A., Shazeer, N., Parmar, N., Uszkoreit, J., Jones, L., Gomez, A.N., Kaiser, Ł., Polosukhin, I.: Attention is all you need. In: Advances in Neural Information Processing Systems, pp. 5998–6008 (2017)
24. Williams, R.J., Zipser, D.: A learning algorithm for continually running fully recurrent neural networks. Neural Comput. **1**(2), 270–280 (1989)
25. Yao, Y., Cao, Y.: A neural network enhanced hidden Markov model for tourism demand forecasting. Appl. Soft Comput. J. **94**(106465), 1–20 (2020)
26. Zhu, J., Song, Y., Zhao, L., Li, H.: A3T-GCN: Attention Temporal Graph Convolutional Network for Traffic Forecasting

Popular and on the Rise—But Not Everywhere: COVID-19-Infographics on Twitter

Benedict Witzenberger⬤, Angelina Voggenreiter⬤, and Jürgen Pfeffer⬤

Abstract The coronavirus pandemic has altered many industries around the world. Journalism is one of them. Especially data journalists have gained attention within and outside of their newsrooms. We aim to study the prevalence of journalistic data visualizations before and after COVID-19 in 1.9 million image posts of news organizations on Twitter across six countries using a semi-manual detection approach. We find an increase in the shares of tweets containing infographics. Although this effect is not consistent across countries, we find increases in the prevalence of COVID-19-related content and interactions in infographics throughout all geographies. This study helps to generalize existing qualitative research on a larger, international scale.

Keywords COVID-19 · Data visualization · Data journalism

1 Introduction

COVID-19 served as an accelerator for ongoing changes in journalism: the decline of print and other forms of "traditional" media, the rise of "alternative" news channels, altered skill requirements for journalists, changes in audience and their expectations [19]. Data journalists were central to some of these innovations, as they had the experience and technical means to create data visualizations and exploratory pieces on possible scenarios, which has increased awareness and accessibility to the numbers and fostered engagement of the audience [17]. We define data journalism as the use of data, quantitative analysis, and visualization methods to create journalism [2].

To shed light on the changes that were going on in journalistic data visualization around the world, we analyzed infographics shared by news media before and after COVID-19 hit as a proxy for the prevalence of data journalism. We define information graphics (short: infographics) as a graphical composition of one or more visualizations based on numerical data, images, and text [4].

We aim to answer the following research questions:

RQ1: How has the use of journalistic infographics changed during COVID-19?
RQ2: Which change in the prevalence of journalistic infographics can be found across different countries?
RQ3: How large is the portion of COVID-19 related infographics?
RQ4: How do tweet interactions change in tweets containing infographics compared to other image tweets?

B. Witzenberger (✉) · A. Voggenreiter · J. Pfeffer
School of Social Sciences and Technology, Technical University of Munich, Munich, Germany
e-mail: benedict.witzenberger@tum.de
URL: https://www.hfp.tum.de/

A. Voggenreiter
e-mail: angelina.voggenreiter@tum.de

J. Pfeffer
e-mail: juergen.pfeffer@tum.de

© The Author(s), under exclusive license to Springer Nature Switzerland AG 2024
P. Haber et al. (eds.), *Data Science—Analytics and Applications*,
https://doi.org/10.1007/978-3-031-42171-6_7

2   Literature Review

We place our research on the influence of infographics in the news and the impact of COVID-19 on data journalism.

Data journalism during COVID-19 Data journalism is regarded as a form of content or genre innovation in journalism [7], which might provide news companies with an increased reputation or a competitive advantage. Demand for data journalistic training has increased, and data journalists have grown in power and reframed their roles and identity in the newsroom [10]. A positive attitude towards data journalism in the newsrooms correlates with enjoying working with numbers and the belief that competency for data work is satisfactory [3].

The number of published data visualizations during COVID-19 led to criticism about an "information overload" [11], a "bombardment" with visualizations [8] and a very small number of sources, as governmental actors were the main data providers during COVID-19 [14]. Journalists use a small set of authoritative sources, which in turn gain authority by being used in media. To stand out, some media outlets performed their own data collection [5].

The general meaningfulness of leveraging COVID-19-related infographics has been examined in the literature. Visual communication can increase the understandability of highly-scientific topics like the spread of a virus for less educated groups [9], and might lead to higher acceptance for and adherence to protection measures. Research on the effects of infographics during COVID-19 could find positive effects on users' knowledge of mask-wearing techniques, and increased trust compared to text-only guidance, but no substantial effect on COVID-19-related anxiety [6]. Others found a positive effect of infographics on the intention to get a COVID-19 vaccination [20].

Infographics, journalism and COVID-19 Infographics are sometimes described as a method to integrate big data into journalism [21], although this does not necessarily points to the volume of data, which might not really be "big", but aspects like variety (of sources and data types) or veracity of information (in comparison to more traditional ways of reporting). Infographics seem to lead to increased news elaboration and increase more favorable news evaluation [12].

There are three common types of infographics–principle representation (or explanatory visualizations, which explain how things work), cartographic infographics (which show where things are), and statistics charts (which show how many things there are) [22]. We only focus on cartographic and statistic charts here, which are based on some form of numeric data, while principle representations are not necessarily grounded on datasets.

Yet, data journalists have been criticized for COVID-19 charts that might "make the world look more 'fixed' than it really is" [16] with maps not accounting for population densities, models not reporting their underlying assumptions, or exclusion of communities at the margins or the Global South [15].

3   Method

To analyze the diffusion of infographics, we collected data from Twitter, which news media uses mainly as a one-way communication channel to promote reporting [13]. We then implemented a semi-manual approach for infographic detection.

Twitter Collection We collected accounts for the five largest, national, general-audience news media across six different countries by circulation: USA, UK, Germany, France, Italy.[1] To allow some variety of cultural backgrounds while still allowing authors to manually code and understand the content, three English-speaking newspapers from India were included. See Appendix A for accounts.

Tweets were retrieved using `from:USERNAME has:images` on Twitter's API v2 [18]. 2,205,025 tweets for this query were collected for the time range between January 1st, 2018, and July 31st, 2022, in the time between August 15th and September 3rd, 2022. However, contrary to the expected returns, not all of these contained images. In total, we could download 1,911,496 images for analysis, either in JPEG or PNG format. The time range was selected to allow comparable time periods before and after the COVID-19 pandemic started.

Identifying Characteristics of Infographics In line with the definition above, we defined infographics as images containing infographic elements, such as diagrams, maps, or explanatory illustrations, as well as text. To be able to detect infographics

---

[1] Sources for circulation numbers: Alliance for Audited Media (USA) via pressgazette.co.uk/news/us-newspaper-circulations-2022, ABC (UK): www.abc.org.uk, IVW e. V. (Germany): www.ivw.de, ACPM (France): www.acpm.fr, FIEG (Italy): www.fieg.it, ABC (India): www.auditbureau.org, RNI: rni.nic.in.

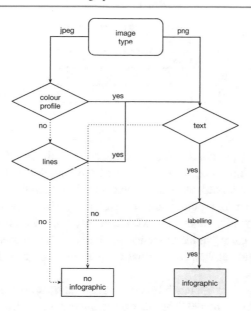

Fig. 1 Infographic detection and labeling process

within our dataset, we first had to define the typical characteristics of an infographic. Therefore, we created a labeled test set consisting of 600 infographics and 1000 non-infographics (as typically more non-infographics than infographics are published by media accounts). The size of the test set allowed us to include a wide variety of images with very different image characteristics, as well as to include non-infographics, which looked very similar to infographics, and vice versa. Using this test set, we identified typical characteristics of infographics and optimized the image characteristic parameters in a way so that **all** infographics of the test set would be extracted (to the price of non-infographics being detected as well):

- **Image type**: If the image was a .png-file, it was likely to be created or edited on a computer and, therefore, likely no common photograph but an image containing graphical elements. For example, 39% of infographics in the test set were PNG-images, while only 14% of non-infographic were PNG-images. We consequently extracted all .png-images [1].
- **Colours**: While photographs typically contain a wide color range, as shadows and light conditions create many different shades of colors in objects, infographics typically consist of a few different graphical elements in a few different colors. It should be noted that transitions between graphical elements can also result in many different color shades, but these colors typically span only a few pixels. We thus extracted all images consisting of few colors spanning a wide area of pixels. In particular, we calculated an RGB histogram of the grayscale image, selected the maximum amount of pixels pix_max one color would span, detected the number of colors n spanning at least one-quarter of pix_max pixels and extracted the image if $n > 30$. While 98% of infographics in the test set fulfilled this attribute, only 55% of non-infographics did so.
- **Edges**: Infographics mostly contain graphical elements such as text boxes or diagram axes, which can be detected by determining the existence of longer lines in the image. Thus, we extracted all images which included a line spanning at least one-sixth of the minimum of the image length and width. While 94% of infographics in the test set contained such a line, only 64% of non-infographics did so as well.

By extracting all images, which would include at least one of these image characteristics, **all** infographics of the test set could be extracted (resulting in 80% of non-infographics being pulled as well).

From these images, we extracted all images which contained text. We used the *pytesseract* optical character recognition package[2] to detect the existence of text within the image, but as sometimes text in specific fonts was not recognized by the system, around 10% of infographics in the test set were excluded by this step. At the same time, this step was crucial to exclude more non-infographics, as 64% of non-infographics in the test set could be excluded after this step.

Labelling Images After identifying the characteristics of an infographic, we applied these to the dataset of Twitter images by using a semi-automatic approach, as illustrated in Fig. 1: First, we extracted all images, including at least one of the infographic

[2] https://pypi.org/project/pytesseract/.

Table 1 Comparison of predicted labels (with semi-automatic approach) versus human-coded, actual labels in a testset with $n = 2500$

Predicted condition	Actual condition	
	Infographics	Non-infographics
Infographics	26	4
Non-Infographics	8	2462

characteristics described above (image type, colors, edges), which reduced the initial dataset of our Twitter images to 71%. Second, we extracted all images containing text, which decreased the complete dataset size to 16% of the initial dataset. Thirdly, as mentioned above, this process would allow us to detect most infographics at the price of extracting a large number of non-infographics as well. These non-infographics had to be excluded by human inspection. Consequently, we distributed the remaining images to four trained human annotators, who manually excluded all images not being an infographic. The annotators were instructed to focus on cartographic or statistical charts, which needed to be grounded on numeric data and were not solely a text containing a single number, but a visual representation of data. The step of manual inspection reduced the dataset size to 1% of the initial size.

Finally, we evaluated this semi-automatic approach by creating a random subset of 2,500 images, labeling these images with the semi-automatic approach (to infer the predicted labels), manually inspecting these images (to infer the true labels), and comparing the labels. Our approach showed a sensitivity of 0.765 (26 out of 34), a specificity of 0.998 (2462 out of 2466), an accuracy of 0.995, and an F1-score of 0.813 (see Table 1).

4   Results

Out of the 1,911,496 images we analyzed, we found 25,813 infographics using the semi-automatic approach described above.

An increase in infographics—but not everywhere The share of infographics within all shared media images increased significantly after the COVID-19 pandemic hit. We defined 'after COVID-19' by tweets published after March 1st, 2020—when the pandemic as a journalistic topic had spread worldwide. We found an increase of 42% between pre- and post-pandemic infographic proportions from 1.2% ($n = 10,652$) to 1.6% ($n = 15,161$) ($\chi^2 = 742.98$, $p < 0.01$, $df = 1$). Still, their share within all images was just around 1.6%, with most images (98.4%) remaining non-infographics. While this seemed to be a clear direction, we found differences when splitting the data into the observed countries.

Not all countries had similar increases in infographics. We found that media in the US had the largest absolute increase of infographics with 2.1 percentage points from 5.7% before the pandemic to 7.8% after. The highest proportional increase was found in India, which increased the share by 130% from 1% to 2.3%. In the UK, we found similar relative growths of around 125%.

In contrast, the share of infographics remained constant in German media at 0.7%. In Italy and France, we found fewer infographics after COVID-19: Italy decreased by around 10% to 1.9%, and in France, the share dropped from 2.8% before COVID-19 to 1.9% after, reducing by around 32%.

COVID-19 is a prominent topic in tweets To further understand the content of the infographics, we analyzed the 50 most-used hashtags for each country. These were manually coded into six categories: COVID-19, politics, ukraine, elections, sports, and others. Ambiguous terms were added to the most distinguishing category ("Biden" to 'elections', "putin" to 'ukraine'). As COVID-19 brought up a set of new, distinctive words, its category seemed very unequivocal.

COVID-19 was found in between 8.1 and 23% of all tweets in our sample after the start of the pandemic. This also holds if only regarding infographics tweets, where COVID-19-related infographics made up 27.8% ($n = 4, 220$) of all 15,161 detected infographics. While everywhere the share of tweets about COVID compared to other topics was higher for non-infographics than for infographics, this difference was very small in France (11.1% infographics, 13% non-infographics COVID-19-related). However, 63% of tweets could not be attributed.

When only regarding infographics after COVID-19 hit, we found that nearly half of infographics in German media were COVID-related, 33.2% in Italy, 30.8% in India, and 26.2% in France (see Fig. 2). The UK and especially the US had smaller shares for COVID-19.

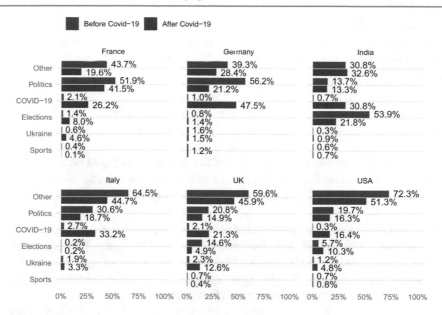

Fig. 2 Share of infographic tweets before and after COVID by clustered topics

Infographic tweets receive higher interactions From a social media perspective, infographics are a valuable tool for media organizations that seek to promote their content via Twitter. We found that mean counts for likes (37.12 versus 66.14), retweets (10.05 versus 28.89), quotes (3.01 versus 6.65), and replies (6.05 versus 7.11) were significantly higher for tweets containing an infographic ($p < 0.001$).

The audience's interest was also visible when comparing infographics before and after COVID-19. We found that after COVID, mean likes (31 versus 90), quotes (5.2 versus 7.6), and replies (4.8 versus 8.7) counts are significantly greater than before ($p < 0.001$). Retweets showed a non-significant increase from 21.2 to 34.3. While we cannot account for changes in followers, as data collection took place at a fixed point in time, we could see that the increases in likes, retweets, and quotes were much higher for infographics than for non-infographics.

5   Discussion

COVID-19 had a solid effect on the prevalence of journalistic infographics on Twitter. We have found an increase in the use of infographics on media's Twitter pages after the start of the COVID-19 pandemic overall, addressing **RQ1**. This increased output of infographics is in line with qualitative literature [8, 11] that labeled these visualizations an "infodemic". Compared to the total number of tweets, however, infographics still only make up a small portion.

For **RQ2**, we found differences between countries. While there were substantial increases for US, Indian, and UK media, stagnation occurred in German media, and we surprisingly found slight declines in France and Italy. We can rule out some possible explanations for this: First, there might be a general difference in the reception of COVID-19 across the studied countries. However, we found much COVID-19-related content when analyzing the infographic tweets' texts across all countries–which also addresses **RQ3**. This leads us to believe that there was a consensus among journalistic infographic designers to produce COVID-19-related content in all observed countries. Second, some media might have different strategies for promoting their content on Twitter. While we cannot control for this from the outside perspective we have taken, we can show for **RQ4** that image tweets containing an infographic receive higher interactions. From a media distribution standpoint, it is rational to use these graphics on Twitter.

Nonetheless third, some media might have different approaches to posting data on social media. While manually labeling the automatically detected infographics, we found "text boards" in many instances. A computational, infographic-like image that contains numbers in textual format, mostly combined with images. These can be regarded as having an infographical appearance and could serve as a substitute for creating charts, which leads to higher requirements for data collection and analysis. From a definitional point of view, we decided not to include these images, as they do not contain charts but only display single numbers. As we only attributed binary labels to the infographics, we cannot control whether this has had a huge influence on the analysis.

6   Limitations

To explain precisely what led to the stagnation in Germany and the decline in Italy and France would require more insights into the newsrooms to rule out editorial decisions which are not visible from the outside. Some qualitative work has already been accomplished around this [5], restricted in scope and generalizability, however, by the efforts that a qualitative study requires.

This study is limited by several factors: Our approach left us relying on Twitter to detect images correctly. As we collected all data at one point in time, tweets that had been deleted could not be used for this study. The focus on six countries might have included strong influences of western-democratic media business that might not be applicable elsewhere. Although Indian media also followed the trend, restricting it to English-speaking media might have influenced the outcome, as others have discovered differences between western democracies and the Global South [14, 15].

Further research might focus on a larger variety of non-western countries to enhance understanding of possible differences in media cultures around the publication of infographics. It might also be beneficial to develop quantitative methods to detect publication differences within certain media markets, which is a field that is mostly covered by qualitative work and is hard to generalize and transfer to other populations.

In addition, our semi-automatic approach was restricted by the quality of text detection. As described in Sect. 3, the existence of text within an image was a critical, required factor in differentiating between infographics and non-infographics, but at the same time, text detection failed in around 10% of infographics. Future research could use more elaborated text detection techniques to also take small, hardly readable, and non-standard texts (e.g., text in the form of word art) into account. This also limits our results which did not include infographics without text, which, however, we only expect to appear in very few cases, as data visualizations usually need some form of textual integration.

7   Conclusion

COVID-19 has influenced innovation in journalism in a lot of ways. We presented a quantitative study on the use of infographics on Twitter before and after COVID-19, which confirms earlier qualitative research. We saw an increase in infographics in our sample of image posts by the largest newsrooms in three of the six researched countries. However, in some countries, they declined. Nonetheless, we found an increase in COVID-19-related content, which is high across all geographies studied for image tweets in general, and infographic tweets in particular. Interactions for infographic tweets are higher than for images. This remains a topic for further research with deeper insights into newsroom practices. News organizations could adapt to COVID-19 in various ways. Increased use of infographics is just one of these developments–and might further influence reporting with potential consequences on the perception of journalism.

Acknowledgements The authors would like to thank Sophie Brandt, Linus Mosch, and Sarah Talbi for their help with labeling the visualizations.

A   Media Accounts

See Table 2.

Table 2 Selected accounts for analysis

Country	Accounts	Followers
France	L'Humanite (@humanite_fr)	396 k
	Le Figaro (@le_figaro)	3.6 m
	Le Monde (@lemondefr)	10.5 m
	Le Parisien (@le_Parisien)	3.2 m
	Liberation (@libe)	3.4 m
Germany	Bild (@BILD)	1.9 m
	Die Welt (@welt)	1.8 m
	Frankfurter Allgemeine (@faznet)	803 k
	Handelsblatt (@handelsblatt)	379 k
	Sueddeutsche Zeitung (@SZ)	1.8 m
India	Hindustan Times (@httweets)	8.6 m
	The Hindu (@the_hindu)	7.9 m
	Times of India (@timesofindia)	14.6 m
Italy	Corriere della Sera (@Corriere)	2.7 m
	Il Resto del Carlino (@qn_carlino)	55 k
	Il Sore 24 Ore (@sole24ore)	1.8 m
	La Reppublica (@repubblica)	3.5 m
	La Stampa (@lastampa)	1.3 m
UK	Daily Mail (@mailonline)	2.8 m
	Daily Mirror (@dailymirror)	1.3 m
	The Daily Telegraph (@telegraph)	3.3 m
	The Sun (@thesun)	2 m
	The Times (@thetimes)	1.7 m
USA	Los Angeles Times (@latimes)	4 m
	New York Times (@nytimes)	54.9 m
	USA Today (@USATODAY)	4.9 m
	Wall Street Journal (@wsj)	20.4 m
	Washington Post (@washingtonpost)	20 m

References

1. Adler, M., Boutell, T., Brunschen, C., Costello, A.M., Crocker, L.D., Dilger, A., Fromme, O., Gailly, J.l., Herborth, C., Jakulin, A., Kettler, N., Lane, T., Lehmann, A., Lilley, C., Martindale, D., Mortensen, O., Pickens, K.S., Poole, R.P., Randers-Pehrson, G., Roelofs, G., van Schaik, W., Schalnat, G., Schmidt, P., Wegner, T., Wohl, J.: PNG (Portable Network Graphics) Specification. Version 1.0. W3C (1996) https://www.w3.org/TR/REC-png-961001

2. Anderton-Yang, D., Kayser-Bril, N., Howard, A., Teixeira, C.V., Slobin, S., Vermanen, J.: Why is data journalism important? In: Gray, J., Bounegru, L., Chambers, L., European Journalism Centre, Open Knowledge Foundation (eds.) The Data Journalism Handbook 1. European Journalism Centre (2012) https://datajournalism.com/read/handbook/one/introduction/why-is-data-journalism-important

3. Appelgren, E., Nygren, G.: Data journalism in Sweden. Digit. J. **2**(3), 394–405 (2014). https://doi.org/10.1080/21670811.2014.884344

4. Cairo, A.: The Functional Art. New Riders Publishing (2012)

5. Desai, A., Nouvellet, P., Bhatia, S., Cori, A., Lassmann, B.: Data journalism and the COVID-19 pandemic: opportunities and challenges. Lancet Digit. Health **3**(10), 619–621 (2021). https://doi.org/10.1016/S2589-7500(21)00178-3

6. Egan, M., Acharya, A., Sounderajah, V., Xu, Y., Mottershaw, A., Phillips, R., Ashrafian, H., Darzi, A.: Evaluating the effect of infographics on public recall, sentiment and willingness to use face masks during the COVID-19 pandemic: a randomised internet-based questionnaire study. BMC Pub. Health **21**(1), 367 (2021). https://doi.org/10.1186/s12889-021-10356-0

7. García-Avilés, J.A.: Reinventing television news: Innovative formats in a social media environment. In: Studies in Big Data, pp. 143–155. Springer International Publishing (2020). https://doi.org/10.1007/978-3-030-36315-4_11

8. García-Avilés, J.A., Arias-Robles, F., de Lara-González, A., Carvajal, M., Valero-Pastor, J.M., Mondéjar, D.: How COVID-19 is revamping journalism: newsroom practices and innovations in a crisis context. J. Pract. 1–19 (2022). https://doi.org/10.1080/17512786.2022.2139744

9. Hamaguchi, R., Nematollahi, S., Minter, D.J.: Picture of a pandemic: visual aids in the COVID-19 crisis. J. Pub. Health **42**(3), 483–485 (2020). https://doi.org/10.1093/pubmed/fdaa080

10. Hermida, A., Young, M.L.: Data Journalism and the Regeneration of News (2019). https://www.routledge.com/Data-Journalism-and-the-Regeneration-of-News/Hermida-Young/p/book/9781138058934

11. Krawczyk, K., Chelkowski, T., Laydon, D.J., Mishra, S., Xifara, D., Gibert, B., Flaxman, S., Mellan, T., Schwämmle, V., Röttger, R., Hadsund, J.T., Bhatt, S.: Quantifying online news media coverage of the COVID-19 pandemic: Text mining study and resource. J. Med. Internet Res. **23**(6), e28253 (2021). https://doi.org/10.2196/28253

12. Lee, E.J., Kim, Y.W.: Effects of infographics on news elaboration, acquisition, and evaluation: Prior knowledge and issue involvement as moderators. New Media Soc. **18**(8), 1579–1598 (2016). https://doi.org/10.1177/1461444814567982

13. Malik, M.M., Pfeffer, J.: A macroscopic analysis of news content in twitter. Digit. J. **4**(8), 955–979 (2016). https://doi.org/10.1080/21670811.2015.1133249

14. Mellado, C., Georgiou, M., Nah, S.: Advancing journalism and communication research: new concepts, theories, and pathways. J. Mass Commun. Quart. **97** (2020). https://doi.org/10.1177/1077699020917204

15. Milan, S., Treré, E.: The rise of the data poor: The COVID-19 pandemic seen from the margins. Soc. Media + Soc. **6**(3) (2020). https://doi.org/10.1177/2056305120948233

16. Northwestern Buffett Institute for Global Affairs: Visualizing a World of COVID-19 Uncertainty (2020) https://buffett.northwestern.edu/news/2020/visualizing-a-world-of-covid-19-uncertainty.html

17. Pentzold, C., Fechner, D.J., Zuber, C.: "Flatten the curve": Data-driven projections and the journalistic brokering of knowledge during the COVID-19 crisis. Digit. J. **9**(9), 1367–1390 (2021). https://doi.org/10.1080/21670811.2021.1950018

18. Pfeffer, J., Mooseder, A., Lasser, J., Hammer, L., Stritzel, O., Garcia, D.: This sample seems to be good enough! assessing coverage and temporal reliability of Twitter's Academic API. In: Proceedings of the Seventeenth International AAAI Conference on Web and Social Media (ICWSM-2023) Forthcoming (2023)

19. Quandt, T., Wahl-Jorgensen, K.: The Coronavirus pandemic and the transformation of (digital) journalism. Digit. J. **10**(6), 923–929 (2022). https://doi.org/10.1080/21670811.2022.2090018

20. Riggs, E.E., Shulman, H.C., Lopez, R.: Using infographics to reduce the negative effects of jargon on intentions to vaccinate against COVID-19. Pub. Understand. Sci. **31**(6), 751–765 (2022). https://doi.org/10.1177/09636625221077385

21. Smit, G., Haan, Y.D., Buijs, L.: Working with or next to each other? boundary crossing in the field of information visualisation. J. Media Innovat. **1**(2), 36–51 (2014). https://doi.org/10.5617/jmi.v1i2.875

22. Zwinger, S., Langer, J., Zeiller, M.: Acceptance and usability of interactive infographics in online newspapers. In: 2017 21st International Conference Information Visualisation (IV). IEEE (2017). https://doi.org/10.1109/iv.2017.65

Taxonomy-Enhanced Document Retrieval with Dense Representations

Victor Mireles⊙, Artem Revenko⊙, Ioanna Lytra⊙, Anna Breit⊙, and Julia Klezl

Abstract Document retrieval is a task that powers several downstream applications such as search and question answering. One way to approach this task is to take embeddings of the documents to be retrieved, and of the query, and use a similarity function to rank results. In this work, we extend this approach by incorporating knowledge about entities mentioned in either the document or the query, in the form of taxonomic relations and canonical labels of said entities. The method, when applied to a domain-specific corpus, improves retrieval recall over a state of the art method trained on a general domain corpus. It does so without requiring any further retraining of the machine learning models involved, thus making it applicable for use cases where training is not feasible because of data or infrastructure limitations.

Keywords Document retrieval · Question answering · Knowledge infusion · Knowledge model · Taxonomy

1 Introduction

Search and Question Answering (QA) engines are widely used in real-world applications by millions of users every day. Both types of engines rely on a method to retrieve documents given a natural language query. Traditionally, TF-IDF or BM25 are used as document-retrieval methodologies. These methodologies match keywords efficiently, and, therefore, can be formalised as operations on very sparse high-dimensional vectors. Conversely, a dense, latent semantic encoding is complementary to sparse representations by design. For example, synonyms or paraphrases that consist of completely different tokens may still be mapped to vectors close to each other. Despite breakthroughs in large language models based on neural networks, dense retrieval methods had never been shown to outperform TF-IDF/BM25 for open domain QA before ORQA [5]. After ORQA, other systems relying on dense representations such as REALM [2] and, especially, DPR [3] have further advanced state of the art results on a wide range of benchmark datasets.

Typically, methodologies relying on dense representations make use of a pre-trained (and, possibly, fine-tuned later) language model (PTLM). Such PTLMs in general work well with data that is similar to the pre-training corpus. Therefore, when the corpus contains a large amount of domain-specific terms or common-usage terms used in domain-specific senses, the implicit semantics of these terms captured by a large language model might be noisy, or non-existent. For example, if a corpus contains many mentions of a product name, or of a specific technology that was not seen during pre-training, these will be treated as a set of sub-word tokens carrying little or no information. However, it is not always feasible to first collect a use-case specific corpus for fine-tuning a large language model.

V. Mireles (✉) · A. Revenko · I. Lytra · A. Breit · J. Klezl
Semantic Web Company GmbH, Vienna, Austria
e-mail: victor.mireles@semantic-web.com

A. Revenko
e-mail: artem.revenko@semantic-web.com

I. Lytra
e-mail: ioanna.lytra@semantic-web.com

A. Breit
e-mail: anna.breit@semantic-web.com

J. Klezl
e-mail: julia.klezl@semantic-web.com

To overcome this issue and enable domain adaptation without re-training we present a method that integrates knowledge from a domain-specific thesaurus into the process of creating document embeddings. Therefore, we enhance a PTLM with external knowledge modelled by experts to come up with a knowledge-enhanced pre-trained language model (KEPTLM), an active area of research [9, 11]. Following [11], our approach would classify as "Entity fused KEPTLMs", with our method of ingesting knowledge is categorised as "Data Structure Unified KEPTMs", similar to K-BERT [6]. In the categorisation introduced in [9], our method falls into the "Encyclopedia Knowledge" (together with LUKE [10], ERNIE [8]) and "Entity Knowledge" (LUKE [10], CoLAKE [7]) categories.

The method we introduce differs from other knowledge infusion methods since it does not require further training of the PTLM, which makes it applicable in scenarios with small corpora or few computing resources.

As a basis for evaluation, we collected a corpus and set of queries from an enterprise setting, and manually generated a dataset of query-document pairs. We compared our approach to several baselines.

2 Example Problem: Retrieving Help Pages

Let us consider the case of a user arriving with a question in mind on the support page of a software product. In this case, the corpus of documents would be the documentation prepared by the software provider.

In this paper, we deal with a corpus consisting of 1107 pages of technical documentation for a specific software product, and a list of 47 real-world questions that users have typed into the search bar of the product's help page. These questions are the result of a manual inspection and selection by experts employed by the software provider, to ensure that for each question there is one help page that fully contains the answer (i.e. it is not necessary to look at two or more documents to find the answer).

The corpus is domain-specific in that it mentions, for example, certain actions that a user must perform on the software's user interface, or certain API calls that they must make. Likewise, since the software in question is mostly used by corporate clients, some of which undergo specific training and certification to use it, it is expected that many domain-specific terms appear in both the questions and the corpus.

To deal with the domain specificity of the example corpus, we use a corporate taxonomy prepared by the software vendor. This taxonomy is part of an enterprise knowledge graph used by the software vendor to organize its internal documentation, of which customer support materials make only a small fraction. It takes the form of a SKOS taxonomy consisting of 11 concept schemes and a total of 1841 concepts. In addition to their canonical (preferred) labels, there are 2459 alternative and 344 hidden labels. The concepts cover organisational information such as departments, roles, document sources within the company, personnel skills, and product-related information such as software components and features, as well as general concepts, industries, and organisations from the domains of where the software vendor is specialised.

The taxonomy was first created for use in the internal Knowledge Hub of the vendor, a semantic search that unifies information from several internal and public data sources.

3 Method

We consider a corpus consisting of a set of documents $\{d_1, d_2, \ldots d_N\}$ and a taxonomy $T = (V, E)$ where entities V represent the graph nodes and E denotes edges which encode taxonomic relationships between entities. Each document d_i contains a set of mentions $\{(v_1, s_1), (v_2, s_2), \ldots (v_{n_d}, s_{n_d})\}$ of the entities in T, where a mention is a tuple (v, s) denoting that entity $v \in V$ is mentioned in the document at character offset s. The task dealt with in this work is, given a query q in natural language, to find the document d_i that best describes the answer to the query.

In this paper, we modify the dense passage retrieval (DPR) method [3] in order to incorporate the knowledge that is contained in the taxonomy. The general approach consists of two parts. The first one, which can be executed offline (before any query arrives), consists of obtaining a vector representation (embedding) of each document d in the corpus and ingesting said representation into a vector database. The second part, which must be executable online (in a timely manner), consists of obtaining a vectorisation of the input query q, and finding the most similar document from the corpus.

Document Embedding Our approach to embedding is a modification of the method employed in DPR [3], which consists of a pair of BERT-based encoders fine-tuned for the task: a document encoder E_p and a question encoder E_q, both of which provide a 768-dimensional embedding of an input text. This embedding is done, as has become standard practice, by taking the representation at the final token of the input sequence. The fine-tuning of these encoders is done explicitly on the document retrieval task, in particular using the Natural Questions (NQ) dataset [4], focusing solely on finding the document that contains the answer to a given question.

In this context, the input t (question or document) to an encoder E must first be converted into a pair of sequences. The first one corresponds to the input sequence of tokens that are to be encoded and is denoted by $K(t) \in \mathbb{K}^n$, where $\mathbb{K}$ is the vocabulary of tokens (and sub-word tokens) of BERT, and n is the model's input sequence length (in this case, $n = 512$). The second sequence corresponds to the positions where each of these tokens occurs and is denoted by $P(t) \in \mathbb{N}^n$. A standard BERT-based encoding produces the sequences $K(t)$ and $P(t)$ using the BERT tokenization algorithm. Given that the number of tokens present in a text is, in general, smaller than n, these sequences are usually right-padded.

Taxonomy exploitation   To incorporate the taxonomical knowledge into the embedding, we first perform entity extraction on the input text t which produces a set of tuples (v_i, s_i) for $i \in \{1, 2, \ldots, v_{n_t}\}$ as defined above. An entity $v \in V$ from the taxonomy has at least two properties that are of interest to us, the first is $L(v)$, a canonical, or preferred label, and the other $B(v) \in V$, another entity which has been marked as semantically broader than v.

Once entity extraction has been performed, we add extra tokens to the input sequence, corresponding to the entities found in the text being embedded. The positions of these tokens are given by the position in which the entity mentions appear, so that the first layer of the BERT encoder receives a position sequence that has, in general, repeated values. This procedure is exemplified in Fig. 1 and explained in detail below.

This strategy of duplicating position indices is similar to the one used in the K-Bert model [6]. Concretely, if we are to add sets of tokens $K_1, K_2, \ldots K_{n_t}$, with each $K_i \subset \mathbb{K}$ corresponding to an entity found in text t at character offset s_i, we would then generate a new token sequence

$$K'(t) = K(t) \oplus K_1 \oplus K_2 \ldots \oplus K_{n_t} \oplus [CLS]$$ (1)

and a position sequence

$$P'(t) = P(t) \oplus [\tau(s_1), \tau(s_1) + 1, \ldots, \tau(s_1) + |K_1|] \oplus \ldots \oplus [\tau(s_{n_t}), \ldots, \tau(s_{n_t}) + |K_{n_t}|]$$ (2)

where τ is a function that converts character offsets into token offsets and $\oplus$ is a sequence concatenation operator that takes into account the maximum input sequence length of the encoder. These token and position sequences are then fed into the encoder to produce a knowledge-infused vector representation of text t.

The extra tokens added can be of two kinds. In the first case, the **canonical labels** $L(v)$ of entities v found in the text are tokenized and the result is added after the tokens of the original sentence. The use of canonical labels helps in identifying different spellings and synonyms of one same entity. It also allows BERT to leverage any semantic information included in the labels when generating the document-wide embedding. The sequence tokens $K_l(t)$ is thus composed by applying Eq. 1 to sets $L(v_1), L(v_2), \ldots L(v_{n_t})$ which result from tokenizing each canonical label individually.

Alternatively, the **labels of broader entities**, $L(B(v))$ can be tokenized and the result added at the end of the tokens of the original sentence. In this way, information that is included in the explicit semantics of the knowledge graph can also be leveraged by the implicit semantics of BERT. In this case, the sequence of tokens $K_b(t)$ is composed by applying Eq. 1 to the sets $L(B(v_1)), L(B(v_2)), \ldots L(B(v_{n_t}))$, which result from tokenizing the canonical labels of the entities broader to the ones found in the text. In the case of multi-hierarchical taxonomies, where a given entity can have more than one broader entity, all of them are included in this list as individual sets. We note that this alternative introduces additional noise in the sequence, as the notion of hypernymy used in the taxonomy can vary in quality and applicability to the given corpus.

Figure 1 exemplifies how canonical labels and labels of broader entities are added into the original token sequence.

Once these sequences of tokens and their corresponding positions have been obtained, they are fed into either of the two encoders, E_p for the documents, E_q for the questions. The output of an encoder for the *CLS* token is considered as the vectorization of said text. In order to enable cosine similarity computations efficiently, the resulting embeddings are L2-normalized before being stored.

Document Similarity Search   As in the original DPR method, finding the most similar document to a question q is performed by finding the document d with the maximum cosine similarity in the embedding space. Furthermore, all documents in the corpus can be ranked with respect to q by sorting them according to said cosine similarity. When the number of documents is

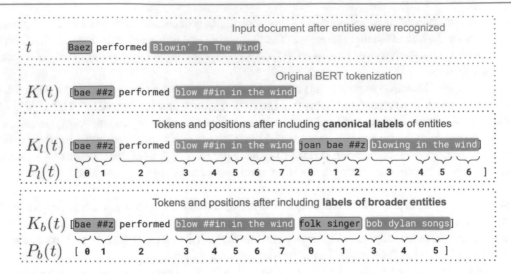

Fig. 1 Construction of the input sequences for a BERT encoder by infusing knowledge contained in a taxonomy. $K_l(t)$ and $P_l(t)$ are the token and position sequences that take into account the canonical labels of entities, and $K_b(t)$ and $P_b(t)$ are the ones that take into account the canonical labels of their broader concepts. See the text for details on how these are computed

large, this operation might require a vector index capable of performing some variation of approximate k nearest neighbors, such as FAISS[1] or Milvus.[2] When the number of documents is small, no approximation is necessary as the distance between $E_q(q)$ and $E_c(d)$ can be computed for every document d.

4   Experiments

We evaluate the method described above on the domain-specific corpus and taxonomy, and a real-world set of questions, described in Sect. 2. Entity extraction from documents was performed using a commercial tool, and the vector similarity computation was done in memory between each question vector and all document vectors, to eliminate possible noise from approximate methods. The BERT-based encoders used were the NQ-corpus pre-trained encoders published in an update to the DPR method.[3] Although these had been fine-tuned for general domain questions, we found that they still provide an advantage over the standard Hugging-face available model of BERT.

Importantly, documents were partitioned into a total of 2524 sections of around 1000 characters each, without breaking tokens apart and, when possible, without dividing text framed by any HTML tag. Since the documents are thus partitioned, the document similarity search defined above will return a ranked set of sections for a given question. Since in the following we report on the ability of the method to retrieve entire documents, we define a document as being in rank r of the results for a given query if r is the smallest rank for one of its sections in the results. Further pre-processing included the removal of URLs and the content of HTML <pre> tags which indicate example code, XML or JSON documents, or command line calls. This pre-processing is especially important in this case because when a document is tokenized by BERT into a very long sequence, there is no further space in the input sequences for the extra tokens representing the knowledge in the taxonomy.

4.1   Results

We evaluate DPR for concept retrieval with and without extra knowledge being incorporated into the document embeddings. The knowledge can be incorporated in two ways: by including the canonical labels for entities mentioned in the text, and by including the canonical labels of their broader entities. We compare these three DPR-based approaches to a baseline

---

Table 1 Results of experiments on the Help Page corpus. Shown is the percentage of correctly-retrieved documents among the top K results for each question

Vectorization	Hits @1	Hits @3	Hits @5	Hits @10
DPR with canonical labels	**0.085**	0.255	**0.404**	**0.574**
DPR with labels of broader entities	0.064	0.191	0.319	0.426
DPR only with text	**0.085**	0.191	0.255	0.532
Baseline TF-IDF	**0.234**	**0.319**	0.340	0.426
HF BERT without fine-tuning, only text	0.000	0.000	0.000	0.021

TF-IDF-based approach that considers only the text in the documents and the questions, as it is a standard method behind many enterprise-search solutions. Finally, we present results with a not-fine-tuned BERT (from the Huggingface (HF) repository of models) using only text, to highlight the advantages of the QA-driven fine-tuning of a language model. Results are presented in Table 1, where the proportion of documents that were correctly retrieved among the top K results for a query ($Hits@K$) is reported. Observing this metric for several values of K allows us to evaluate the effect of the embedding proposed on the ranking of documents as they are being retrieved. Correctly-ranked document retrieval is, in general, a hard task, and the results of state of the art methods without corpus-specific fine-tuning is comparably low to those reported here.

It is clear from the results that in this domain-specific scenario, infusing text embeddings with knowledge from a taxonomy is beneficial to the document retrieval task. While the results are worse than those reported in [3] for a general-domain corpus for which the DPR encoders were originally trained, the results are better than those reported with DPR specifically fine-tuned for a domain-specific corpus of 4415 documents [1]. In summary, we have taken a model trained on a different dataset and improved its performance on this domain-specific dataset without further training.

5   Conclusion and Next Steps

This work shows how to integrate knowledge contained in a taxonomy into a document retrieval system, without the need for further training of any machine learning models. The results—although modest in terms of percentage of correct pages retrieved in the top 10 results—are an improvement over the use of an off-the-shelf DPR encoder. This shows that the use of taxonomies brings an advantage when generating embeddings, even when exploiting only the information contained in the labels of the entities.

It is important to note that the results presented here were computed using a domain-specific taxonomy on a domain-specific corpus. This means that the datasets themselves are not further applicable, but it is rather the method that can be reused to enhance document retrieval in domain-specific scenarios where a taxonomy is available.

One direction of future work includes using a general-domain Knowledge Graph, such as Wikidata, to perform entity extraction on a general-domain corpus. Additionally, the integration of knowledge other than the labels and hypernym labels to further improve the results are of great interest.

The method presented here, as all BERT-based methods, rely heavily on the token embedding step, which is based on a fixed vocabulary. Since domain-specific use cases might not involve enough data to fine-tune this embeddings, and sub-token embeddings contain little information, it would be advantageous to generate richer embeddings from the Knowledge Graph. Therefore, another direction of future work is the integration of Graph Embeddings into the document retrieval process.

Acknowledgements This work was done in terms of the PORQUE project (https://porque-project.eu/), and funded the Eureka Eurostars programme, Grant Number E114154.

References

1. Althammer, S., Askari, A., Verberne, S., Hanbury, A.: Dossier@ coliee 2021: leveraging dense retrieval and summarization-based re-ranking for case law retrieval. In: Proceedings of the Eighth International Competition on Legal Information Extraction/entailment (COLIEE 2021), pp. 8–14 (2021)

2. Guu, K., Lee, K., Tung, Z., Pasupat, P., Chang, M.W.: REALM: Retrieval-Augmented Language Model Pre-Training. arXiv e-prints arXiv:2002.08909 (Feb 2020). https://doi.org/10.48550/arXiv.2002.08909

3. Karpukhin, V., Oğuz, B., Min, S., Lewis, P., Wu, L., Edunov, S., Chen, D., Yih, W.T.: Dense Passage Retrieval for Open-Domain Question Answering. arXiv e-prints arXiv:2004.04906 (Apr 2020). https://doi.org/10.48550/arXiv.2004.04906

4. Kwiatkowski, T., Palomaki, J., Redfield, O., Collins, M., Parikh, A., Alberti, C., Epstein, D., Polosukhin, I., Devlin, J., Lee, K., et al.: Natural questions: a benchmark for question answering research. Trans. Assoc. Comput. Linguist. **7**, 453–466 (2019)

5. Lee, K., Chang, M.W., Toutanova, K.: Latent retrieval for weakly supervised open domain question answering. In: Proceedings of the 57th Annual Meeting of the Association for Computational Linguistics, pp. 6086–6096. Association for Computational Linguistics, Florence, Italy (Jul 2019). https://doi.org/10.18653/v1/P19-1612

6. Liu, W., Zhou, P., Zhao, Z., Wang, Z., Ju, Q., Deng, H., Wang, P.: K-bert: enabling language representation with knowledge graph. In: Proceedings of the AAAI Conference on Artificial Intelligence, vol. 34, pp. 2901–2908 (2020)

7. Sun, T., Shao, Y., Qiu, X., Guo, Q., Hu, Y., Huang, X., Zhang, Z.: CoLAKE: Contextualized Language and Knowledge Embedding. arXiv e-prints arXiv:2010.00309 (Oct 2020). https://doi.org/10.48550/arXiv.2010.00309

8. Sun, Y., Wang, S., Li, Y., Feng, S., Chen, X., Zhang, H., Tian, X., Zhu, D., Tian, H., Wu, H.: ERNIE: Enhanced Representation through Knowledge Integration. arXiv e-prints arXiv:1904.09223 (Apr 2019). https://doi.org/10.48550/arXiv.1904.09223

9. Wei, X., Wang, S., Zhang, D., Bhatia, P., Arnold, A.: Knowledge Enhanced Pretrained Language Models: A Comprehensive Survey. arXiv e-prints arXiv:2110.08455 (Oct 2021). https://doi.org/10.48550/arXiv.2110.08455

10. Yamada, I., Asai, A., Shindo, H., Takeda, H., Matsumoto, Y.: LUKE: Deep Contextualized Entity Representations with Entity-aware Self-attention. arXiv e-prints arXiv:2010.01057 (Oct 2020). https://doi.org/10.48550/arXiv.2010.01057

11. Yang, J., Xiao, G., Shen, Y., Jiang, W., Hu, X., Zhang, Y., Peng, J.: A Survey of Knowledge Enhanced Pre-trained Models. arXiv e-prints arXiv:2110.00269 (Oct 2021). https://doi.org/10.48550/arXiv.2110.00269

Robustness of Sentiment Analysis of Multilingual Twitter Postings

Beatrice Steiner⊙, Alexander Buchelt⊙, and Alexander Adrowitzer⊙

Abstract Due to increasing digitalisation and access to content published online, the amount of data continues to grow. Opinions, experiences and thoughts are shared on various online platforms. In particular, sharing personal content on social media has become increasingly popular in recent years. Mostly, microblogging is done on social media using text. This text data can be further processed. Information can be extracted from the posted text. Often, a so-called sentiment analysis is used, to determine whether texts adopt a positive, neutral, or negative attitude. Such analysis can be relevant for politics, marketing or economics. Whenever text of a different origin language is to be analysed, a translation to English has to be made beforehand, since sentiment analyses are primarily designed for English text. The necessity for translation poses the question of an introduction of bias towards a particular sentiment, through machine translation. This work shows that for two different architectures of transformer network-based translations, only minimal changes are detectable. This is proved with examples from different origin languages.

Keywords Multilingual sentiment analysis · Social media · Twitter

---

1   Introduction

Social media has grown in popularity over the past decade and today it is impossible to imagine life without it. Users write about a wide variety of topics and express opinions on them. These texts can be categorised in positive, negative or neutral sentiment directions, which can be relevant for different application areas in a broader context. Sentiment analysis, which is part of the field of Natural Language Processing (NLP), provides an automated way to determine the sentiment direction of texts and to use them for further purposes.

Text data from various sources such as social media, newspapers or articles should be treated differently [2]. Widely used fields of application are sociology, marketing, advertising, psychology, economics and politics. Unlike normal texts, there are challenges regarding short texts and their inherently reduced context. In addition, abbreviations and incorrect spelling are often used. [8]. With the widespread use of social media, there is an extensive daily data set of opinions and reviews. Since Twitter is available in many different languages and posts are made in even more languages, it is necessary to provide sentiment analysis methods that support different languages [2].

Machine translation is a common way to address the challenge of different languages. Freely available translation models (e.g., from Google or Bing) have gained accuracy in recent years [4]. Translation can introduce biases towards negative or positive directions of content. This raises the question of whether the original sentiments contained in tweets are still present after translation. This work sets its primary focus on showing robustness within sentiment analysis of automatically

B. Steiner · A. Buchelt · A. Adrowitzer (✉)
Department Computer Science and Security, St. Poelten University of Applied Sciences, Saint Poelten, Austria
e-mail: alexander.adrowitzer@fhstp.ac.at

B. Steiner
e-mail: ds201017@fhstp.ac.at

A. Buchelt
e-mail: alexander.buchelt@fhstp.ac.at

A. Buchelt
Human-Centered AI Lab, Institute of Forest Engineering, University of Natural Resources and Life Sciences Vienna, Vienna, Austria

translated content. Therefore existing analyses are extended by studying machine text translation and sentiment analysis through transformer based models.

The structure of this paper is as follows: Section 2 provides an overview of related work in this field. The dataset used in this study and the prepocessing steps as well as the model architecture are explained in Sect. 3 while Sect. 4 presents the main results. Finally, Sect. 5 concludes our work and discusses future work.

2   Related Work

There exists much literature on sentiment analysis, especially for tweets. Barreto et al. [5] evaluate different language models for sentiment analysis in tweets, including latest approaches such as Transformer-based autoencoder models. Abdullah et al. [1] describe various approaches to multilingual sentiment analysis, including the machine translation approach to text.

Balahur et al. [3] attempted to use statistical machine translation to generate training data in languages other than English and then train models on it. English texts were translated into German, Spanish, and French using Google Translate, Bing Translator, and Moses. Various experiments show that translating training data into other languages using statistical machine translation is sufficient to produce equivalent sentiment analysis models as in the source language, English.

A paper by Shalunts et al. [14] investigates the quality of a sentiment analysis applied to a translated English corpus. The data's original languages in the news domain are German, Russian, and Spanish. The machine translation system SDL Language Waver is used for the translation. The result of their work is the SentiSAIL model.

Poncelas et al. [12] look at the impact of machine translation on sentiment analysis. The dataset includes feedback from clients. In addition, the work deals with the effects of indirect translations (e.g., German to English to German). The feedback is processed using a transformer network from Klein et al. [9] to translate French, Spanish, and Japanese to/from English.

Due to the fact that research in sentiment analysis is mainly conducted in English, Mohammad et al. [10] propose two basic concepts. First, it is a way to translate the texts of a poorly supported language into English. Second, it is a way to translate pre-classified corpora and sentiment lexica from English to a little-supported language. Arabic texts are translated into English (manually and automatically). The English text is then assigned a sentiment (manually and automatically). The sentiment assigned to the translated English text is then compared with the manual sentiment of the Arabic texts. The higher the match rate, the less the translation influences the sentiment.

3   Methodology

3.1   Dataset and Preprocessing

There are various requirements for the data to be used in our experiments. First of all the tweets have to be pre-classified in terms of their sentiment. Furthermore it is important that not only English tweets are included in the data set–a data set with as many different languages as possible is preferred, so that the different translation algorithms can be evaluated. Since the main purpose of this work is to investigate the robustness of machine translated texts with respect to the sentiments and not a sentiment analysis itself, we need a multilingual dataset with sentiments. We chose the "Multilingual Sentiment Dataset", which is provided by Sascha Narr from the Technical University of Berlin, Germany,[1] for this purpose. Narr collected 12591 tweets in four different languages: English, German, French and Portuguese, and used the Amazon Mechanical Turk platform for annotation. Each tweet was annotated by three different workers. The sentiment of the tweets is labeled as positive, negative, neutral or na (for irrelevant or unclear). Some sample tweets are shown in Table 1. He further split the dataset to single files for each language and created special files where all three workers annotated the tweets with the same sentiment (e.g., all three workers annotated a tweet as "positive"). Table 2 shows the different number of tweets among the languages and how many tweets have an agreement of all three workers.

In this work we will use the datasets with complete agreement in the languages English and German, because they are the largest ones and the authors speak both languages. This limitation of data was made so that the authors are able to verify and identify possible misclassifications. The respective files are called *en_sentiment_agree3.tsv* and *de_sentiment_agree3.tsv*.

The following preprocessing steps were applied to the dataset: converting multiple spaces to one space, converting entire tweets to lowercase, removing URLs, removal of numbers, and application of lemmatisation.

---

[1] http://dainas.aot.tu-berlin.de/~andreas@dai/sentiment/.

Table 1 Example tweets for each sentiment label

Sentiment	Tweet
Positive	Fist of Legend was good; but have to agree nothing could beat the first action sequence. It was a good way to start the day.
Negative	The last place i want to be right now when i feel like shit is theatre class.. #IWantMyBed
Neutral	Hello does anyone know how to put audio device back on a sony vaio?
Na	Aii dear am arund.RT @uchygucci: aww.. Meanin ur in dt ur aunts place.. We wd see mao hpfuly..RT @user @user was @user dis aftrn..

Table 2 The total number of tweets (N) and the number of tweets with complete agreement (N_{ca}) of all three workers per language

Language	N	N_{ca}
English	7197	3771
German	1797	958
Portuguese	1799	715
French	1798	688

3.2 Transformer Networks and Sentiment Analysis

To use Transformer Networks for machine translation in the analytical context of an algorithmic bias, there are several requirements to be considered when selecting current models.

A first aspect is that the models can translate from German to English, since most sentiment analysis approaches are designed for English. For Architecture II it is essential that the translation by means of an algorithm from English to the intermediate language German is possible and a further back translation from German to English.

These requirements are met by two algorithms that are suited for our tasks: opus-mt-de-en[2] (short Helsinki) of the University of Helsinki and wmt19-de-en [11] (short Facebook). Another reason why we chose these particular algorithms is that they are open source and free to use.

For sentiment analysis we use the pysentimiento model, which also works with a transformer network. It is an open source Python library for multilingual sentiment analysis and other NLP tasks [13]. The output are the labels POS, NEG, NEU for positive, negative and neutral sentiments respectively.

3.3 Translation Architectures

The first architecture (Architecture I, shown in Fig. 1) is used to compare the two different transformer networks (Helsinki and Facebook) for translation of the tweets to determine if there are substantial differences between the networks. It consists of the following main steps:

1. Translation of the tweets for German to Englisch (GER-ENG).
2. Calculation of the sentiment of the translated tweets with Pysentimiento.
3. Creation of a confusion matrix with original sentiments (rows) and calculated sentiments (columns).

The second architecture (Architecture II, shown in Fig. 2) tests whether the repeated application of transformer networks to make translation has any impact on sentiment. To make the results comparable, this time we do not take the sentiment classification from the original dataset, but the English tweets are also provided with sentiments by pysentimiento. In the evaluation, the sentiments of the tweets before the application of the transformer networks and afterwards are compared. This architecture consists of the following main steps:

---

[2] https://huggingface.co/Helsinki-NLP/opus-mt-de-en.

Fig. 1 Architecture I: German tweets (GER) are translated to English (ENG) with Helsinki and Facebook Model. A sentiment is calculated for the translated tweets and compared with the sentiment of the original tweets

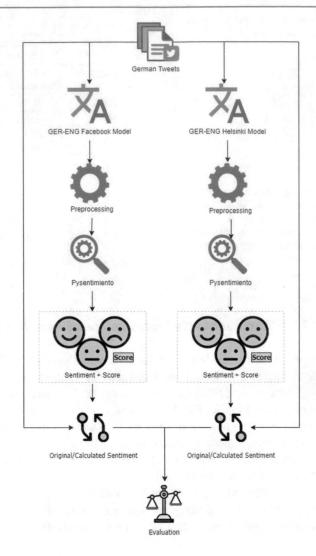

1. Calculation of the sentiment of the original tweets with pysentimiento.
2. Translation of the tweets from English to German.
3. Translation of the tweets from German back to English.
4. Calculation of the sentiment of the translated tweets with pysentimiento.
5. Creation of a confusion matrix with pysentimiento sentiments of the original tweets (rows) and the pysentimiento sentiments of the translated-backtranslated tweets (columns).

We also want to check if the order in which the proposed models are applied influences the stability of the sentiments. To this end, all four combinations (Helsinki-Helsinki, Facebook-Facebook, Helsinki-Facebook and Facebook-Helsinki) are evaluated.

4   Results

To evaluate the results we use two standard metrics. The first one is the Accuracy which represents the proportion of correctly identified tweets to the total number of tweets. The second metric is Cohen's Kappa (κ) [6], which was originally introduced in the area of pyschology to measure the level of agreement between two or more judges on different categories. It is defined as

$$\kappa = \frac{p_a - p_c}{1 - p_c} \tag{1}$$

Fig. 2 Architecture II:
English Tweets are translated
to German (ENG-GER) and
then back to English
(GER-ENG). In the left
branch, the sentiment is
calculated after
translation-backtranslation,
in the right branch the
sentiment is calculated for
the original tweets

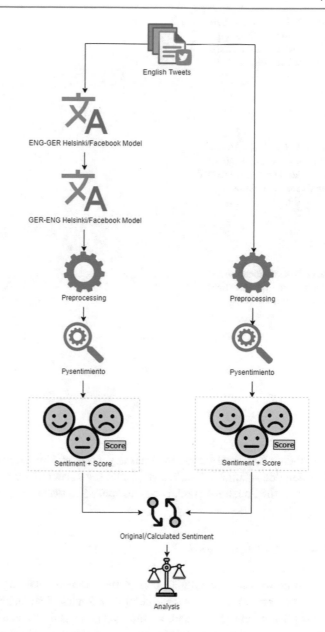

where p_a is the proportion of units where the judges agreed and p_c is the proportion of units where the agreement is expected by chance. Thus, a value of $\kappa = 1$ means total agreement of both judges, $\kappa = 0$ means an agreement by chance. When the κ agreement is less than chance (i.e., $p_a < p_c$), κ will be negative. In classification settings, Cohen's Kappa is used to measure the degree of agreement between the true values and the predicted values. In the multiclass case, p_a is the accuracy of the confusion matrix and p_c can be calculated as

$$p_c = \frac{1}{N^2} \sum_k n_{k_1} n_{k_2},$$
(2)

where N is the total number of instances, n_{k_1} is the number of times judge 1 classified an item as belonging to class k and n_{k_2} is the number of times judge 2 classified an item as belonging to class k [7].

4.1 Architecture I

We used 918 tweets from the German part of the multilingual twitter dataset for the Architecture I analysis. Among them are 140 positive, 93 negative and 685 neutral tweets. Both the Helsinki and the Facebook model achieved a representative value

Table 3 Confusion matrix Helsinki model. Original values are in rows, calculated values are in columns

	NEG	NEU	POS	Total
NEG	65	24	4	93
NEU	62	547	76	685
POS	4	40	96	140
Total	131	611	176	918

Table 4 Confusion matrix Facebook model. Original values are in rows, calculated values are in columns

	NEG	NEU	POS	Total
NEG	67	25	1	93
NEU	72	539	73	684
POS	6	36	97	139
Total	145	600	171	916

Table 5 Classification accuracy and model reliability for the different models

Model	Accuracy	Cohen's kappa
Helsinki–Helsinki	0.915	0.851
Facebook–Facebook	0.920	0.861
Helsinki–Facebook	0.926	0.870
Facebook–Helsinki	0.908	0.841

of Cohen's Kappa of 0.502. In Accuracy, both are similar, Helsinki is slightly better with 0.771 than Facebook with 0.767. The detailed results for the Helsinki and the Facebook model can be found in Tables 3 and 4 respectively. The confusion matrix of the Facebook model contains only 916 tweets, because 2 tweets could not be translated by this model.

4.2 Architecture II

This time we used the english part of the dataset containing 964 tweets with positive sentiment, 658 tweets with negative sentiment and 2138 tweets with neutral sentiment. The results of the evaluations of all combinations of translation models are shown in Table 5. We can see that Accuracy and Cohen's Kappa are all above 0.9 and 0.8 respectively which indicates a very high stability regarding the sentiments of tweets to different translation models. With the choice of this specific datasets there is a slightly better result of Helsinki–Facebook over Facebook–Helsinki but this can not be generalised to other cases.

5 Conclusion and Future Work

In this paper, we showed that modern transformer network-based intelligent translation methods do not influence the sentiments of tweets to a non-acceptable degree. Whether content was translated from various origin languages to English or translation was made sequentially and then translated back to English did not make any meaningful differences. It follows that transformer network-based translations made on social media postings do not alter the original meaning drastically. This builds a solid foundation for proving robustness.

In future work the concept can be extended to more languages and specific use cases, for example product reviews, manuals or comments made on digital video content. Another avenue that is worth exploring is explainability of these concepts. With larger implementation of sentiment analysis, transformer-based artificial intelligence and large language models, understanding exactly how classifications are made, becomes likewise increasingly important.

References

1. Abdullah, N.A.S., Rusli, N.I.A.: Multilingual sentiment analysis: A systematic literature review. Pertanika J. Sci. Technol. **29**, 445–470 (2021). https://doi.org/10.47836/pjst.29.1.25
2. Balahur, A.: Sentiment analysis in social media texts. In: Proceedings of the 4th Workshop on Computational Approaches to Subjectivity, Sentiment and Social Media Analysis, pp. 120–128 (2013). https://aclanthology.org/W13-1617.pdf
3. Balahur, A., Turchi, M.: Multilingual sentiment analysis using machine translation? In: Proceedings of the 3rd Workshop in Computational Approaches to Subjectivity and Sentiment Analysis, pp. 52–60. Association for Computational Linguistics, Jeju, Korea (2012). https://aclanthology.org/W12-3709
4. Balahur, A., Turchi, M.: Comparative experiments using supervised learning and machine translation for multilingual sentiment analysis. Comput. Speech Lang. **28**(1), 56–75 (2014). https://doi.org/10.1016/j.csl.2013.03.004
5. Barreto, S., Moura, R., Carvalho, J., Paes, A., Plastino, A.: Sentiment analysis in tweets: an assessment study from classical to modern word representation models. Data Min. Knowl. Disc. **37**(1), 318–380 (2023). https://doi.org/10.1007/s10618-022-00853-0
6. Cohen, J.: A coefficient of agreement for nominal scales. Educ. Psychol. Measur. **20**(1), 37–46 (1960). https://doi.org/10.1177/001316446002000104
7. Fleiss, J.L., Levin, B., Paik, M.C., et al.: The Measurement of Interrater Agreement, vol. 2. Citeseer (1981)
8. Hutto, C., Gilbert, E.: VADER: A parsimonious rule-based model for sentiment analysis of social media text. Proceed. Int. AAAI Conf. Web Soc. Media **8**(1), 216–225 (2014). https://ojs.aaai.org/index.php/ICWSM/article/view/14550
9. Klein, G., Kim, Y., Deng, Y., Senellart, J., Rush, A.M.: Opennmt: Open-source toolkit for neural machine translation. CoRR arXiv:1701.02810 (2017). http://arxiv.org/abs/1701.02810
10. Mohammad, S.M., Salameh, M., Kiritchenko, S.: How translation alters sentiment. J. Artif. Intell. Res. **55**(1), 95–130 (2016). https://doi.org/10.1613/jair.4787
11. Ng, N., Yee, K., Baevski, A., Ott, M., Auli, M., Edunov, S.: Facebook fair's wmt19 news translation task submission. In: Proceedings of the Fourth Conference on Machine Translation (WMT), pp. 314–319. Curran Associates (2019). https://doi.org/10.48550/arXiv.1907.06616
12. Poncelas, A., Lohar, P., Way, A., Hadley, J.: The impact of indirect machine translation on sentiment classification. CoRR abs/2008.11257 (2020). https://arxiv.org/abs/2008.11257
13. Pérez, J.M., Giudici, J.C., Luque, F.: Pysentimiento: A Python Toolkit for Sentiment Analysis and Socialnlp Tasks (2021). https://github.com/pysentimiento/pysentimiento
14. Shalunts, G., Backfried, G., Commeignes, N.: The impact of machine translation on sentiment analysis. Data Anal. **63**, 51–56 (2016). https://biblio.ugent.be/publication/8116621/file/8132035#page=64

Exploratory Analysis of the Applicability of Formalised Knowledge to Personal Experience Narration

Victor Mireles⬭, Stephanie Billib, Artem Revenko⬭, Stefan Jänicke⬭, Frank Uiterwaal⬭, and Pavel Pecina⬭

Abstract Some of the victims of Nazi prosecution have consigned their personal experiences in the form of diaries of their internment in concentration camps. Such human-centric texts may contrast with the organisation of knowledge about such events that, for example, historians and archivists make. In this work, we analyse six such narrations with the use of Entity Extraction and Named Entity Recognition techniques, present the results of the corresponding exploration, and discuss the suitability of such tools on this corpus. We show that knowledge tools, that have been successfully used to organise documents, can be lacking when describing personal accounts, and we suggest ways to alleviate this.

Keywords Named entity recognition · Entity extraction · Holocaust studies · Knowledge graphs · Digital humanities

1 Introduction

The preservation and study of the memory of crimes against humanity are necessary to maintain a societal consciousness of past atrocities, their organisation, and their preceding developments. Only in this way can future generations identify promptly and counteract any repetition of such tragedies. It is thus understandable and fortunate that the study of such events remains the focus of professionals and the general public.

In the particular case of the victims of Nazi prosecution, this study can start from firsthand accounts of the events, both retrospective and contemporary. These accounts are, for the most part, centred on the human experience of the tragedy and the everyday lives of the participants. This is in contrast with the historiographic tradition, which often focuses on longer periods of time or on events involving large groups of people.

Historiography relies heavily on the organisation of information, the clear definition of concepts, and the abstraction of events, people, and places into categories. With the advent of digital technologies, this organisation has taken on new forms and has been aided by the methods of Natural Language Processing and Information Extraction, among others.

V. Mireles (✉) · A. Revenko
Semantic Web Company GmbH, Vienna, Austria
e-mail: victor.mireles@semantic-web.com

A. Revenko
e-mail: artem.revenko@semantic-web.com

S. Billib
Bergen-Belsen Memorial, Lohheide, Germany
e-mail: stephanie.billib@stiftung-ng.de

S. Jänicke
Department of Mathematics and Computer Science, University of Southern Denmark, Odense, Denmark
e-mail: stjaenicke@imada.sdu.dk

F. Uiterwaal
NIOD, Institute for War, Holocaust and Genocide Studies, Amsterdam, The Netherlands
e-mail: f.uiterwaal@niod.knaw.nl

P. Pecina
Faculty of Mathematics and Physics, Charles University, Prague, Czech Republic
e-mail: pecina@ufal.mff.cuni.cz

© The Author(s), under exclusive license to Springer Nature Switzerland AG 2024
P. Haber et al. (eds.), *Data Science—Analytics and Applications*,
https://doi.org/10.1007/978-3-031-42171-6_10

The creation of these formalised knowledge systems, in the form of ontologies, taxonomies, and knowledge graphs, is increasingly recognised as necessary for the organisation of large masses of sources. In the context of the modern period, knowledge graphs of different types have been built for describing, e.g., the Finnish winter and continuation wars [5], or the history of cities [8], as well as cataloguing important concepts in the history of WW2 and the Holocaust [12].

This structured information is typically made accessible to domain scholars through user interfaces, and the utility and impact of such frameworks [17] and their underlying methodologies are well documented in a recent survey on visualisation strategies for cultural heritage collections [18]. Casual users or domain experts are enabled to analyse large text corpora from different angles, follow down patterns they find interesting, and inspect details on data items suitably contextualised. In addition to such visual analytical environments that support information seeking, digital storytelling [16] has been proven beneficial for exploring and narrating cultural heritage data [9].

A large diversity of exploration means exists particularly for text-based data sources [6], including ego documents like letters [2] or diaries [7]. The latter project on exploring the diaries of the Bergen-Belsen concentration camp revealed the potential but also limitations of current approaches to quantitatively analyse such sensitive data resources. For example, state-of-the-art approaches for sentiment analysis, usually trained on modern texts [11], can hardly extract the emotion in these diaries. For the same reason, the accuracy of named entities depicting persons or geospatial references is insufficient and calls for new methods for automated named entity extraction.

There have been successful applications of Named Entity Recognition techniques which are specifically tuned for historical documents, such as hmBert [15] for German, English, French, Swedish, and Finnish, the work of Rovera et al. [14] for Italian, or that of Hubkova and Král [3] for Czech. Furthermore, systems that work beyond text and incorporate phonetic information for audio recordings have also been produced (e.g., Psutka et al. [13]). For a further survey focused on early-modern materials, the reader is referred to [4]. These methods and their successes can very well complement the formalised knowledge systems such as ontologies and taxonomies, to power the rich information organisation and exploration described above.

This work is an exploration of the commonalities and differences between human-centred accounts of daily life and the historiographic organisation of knowledge about the same historical context. We do this by analysing diaries written by people interned in a Nazi concentration camp using expert-generated vocabularies about WW2 and Named Entity Recognition tools.

2   Datasets

In this work, we process a corpus consisting of six diaries of people interned in the Bergen-Belsen concentration camp. Since life inside Bergen-Belsen is not well documented, prisoner-written texts like diaries are important sources. The different backgrounds (in terms of, for example, age, gender or nationality) of prisoners result in situations or events being described with different languages and interpreted in different forms. The wider the distribution of author backgrounds, the better equipped are historians to highlight the personal perspectives, and to estimate the details of the actual event. The six diaries chosen here cover a broad range of perspectives regarding nationality, gender, age, language, and duration. Among the authors are two female and four male authors, the youngest being 16 years and the oldest 46 years old at the time of liberation. Four authors were imprisoned in the same sub-camp (Star camp), while one author was a prisoner of the Hungarians' camp and one in the Special camp for Polish prisoners.

Three of the six diaries are kept until the time of the liberation in April 1945, the earliest of them starting in October 1943 and thus covering the longest time span of $2\frac{1}{2}$ years. The shortest diary covers four months only. All diaries are handwritten and original languages range from Dutch to Greek, German, Hungarian, Polish and Serbian reflecting the background of their author. Here, we use a digital version of said diaries, specifically of their German-language editions which comprise, in total, 228245 tokens. While only one of them was originally written in German, this is the language of researchers and visitors at the Bergen-Belsen memorial, and therefore most sources are translated by experts into German.

The diaries deal with daily life in the Bergen-Belsen concentration camp. Different aspects of camp life are described and interpreted from the perspective of the three different sub-camps showing different conditions and rules in each of them. A common topic in all the diaries is hunger and the lack of food as well as the social behaviour in the authors' surrounding. In all six diaries the vocabulary is informal but rich with general terms related to Nazi persecution and concentration camps. In addition, there are words used in Bergen-Belsen specifically or even in one of the sub-camps only.

We compare these human-centred documents with a formalisation of the domain done for historiographic purposes, the WW2 Thesaurus.[1] This thesaurus has, over the past decade, become the glue that holds together digital collections with a

---

[1] NIOD website on the WW2 thesaurus. URL: https://www.niod.nl/en/collections/ww2-thesaurus (last accessed on 3 January 2023).

thematic relation to the Second World War. It originated in 2016 when the Dutch NIOD Institute for War, Holocaust, and Genocide Studies transformed the collection of subject headings that it had built, into a semantic graph of meaningful relations. The thesaurus includes over two thousand entities including events, persons, organisations, camps, and juridical concepts [12]. It has been used, for example, to catalogue over a million historical sources in Oorlogsbronnen.[2]

The thesaurus currently contains 6,135 entities with 17,646 SKOS-XL[3] labels in Dutch, German, and English. More entities and labels are constantly added through a community process coupled with expert curation, and linking to Wikidata and Geocodes allows for interoperability with the wider Semantic Web. Because no two entities have the same label, this thesaurus can be used in entity extraction without the need for disambiguation.

The structure of the thesaurus is multi-hierarchical, with entities related to one another through broader/narrower relations indicating some notion of hypernymy. For example, events can be grouped by the year in which they happened, by the type of event (e.g., Attack, Evacuation, Mass executions), or by some other categorisation. This hierarchical structure has a depth of up to 8 levels deep in some cases. The top categories, known as Concept Schemes, are: Organisations, Events, Interment Camps, Places, and General Concepts. They contain, respectively 1431, 1489, 1629, 443, and 5676 different entities.

3   Methods

The exploratory analysis presented here is the result of applying two methods: Entity Extraction and Named Entity Recognition (NER). Entity Extraction (also known as Concept Extraction, or Entity Linking) is the task of identifying mentions of entities from a controlled vocabulary (the WW2 Thesaurus) in a text. In this work, entity extraction was done using a commercial tool[4] that is tolerant to basic inflections of the German language. Since in the thesaurus used in this work, it is often the case that entities have multiple (alternative) labels, entity extraction has the effect of normalising entity mentions. This process results in a set of *concept matches*, which indicate the id of the entity identified, the character offset where it appeared, and the text that the tool deemed as matching text.

For NER we used a German BERT model fine-tuned on the GermEval14 dataset [1] to recognise mentions of named entities. The model is publicly available[5] and the authors report strict F_1 scores of 86.89 and 85.52 on the manually annotated GermEval 2014 and German CoNLL-2003 test data-sets, respectively.[6] Although specialised models [15] have shown better results (in terms of the F_1 score) on historic data sets, the chosen model is only a few points behind state of the art and outperforms specialised models in non-historic corpora. As our corpus contains documents written in modern German we opt for the German BERT model. The model recognises the "big four" NER classes: LOC (Locations), ORG (Organizations), PER (People), OTH (Other). The model also recognises nested entities, however, at this stage of analysis we considered only the larger of the nested entities. The *Named Entity Matches* which result from this process are not normalised, in the sense that two different matches might refer to the same real-world entity being mentioned using different names or, simply, different linguistic variants (e.g., declensions of case).

4   Results

The data-set consisting of the diaries of six inmates of the Bergen-Belsen concentration camp was analysed using two different approaches: entity extraction and named entity recognition. While the former is based on expert-curated knowledge in the form of a thesaurus, so that entities of interest to historians are identified, the latter aims at identifying entities based on the lexical patterns in text. We present the results from each of the methods, and compare them to find commonalities.

---

[2] Oorlogsbronnen website: https://www.oorlogsbronnen.nl/ (last accessed on 3 January 2023).

[3] Simple Knowledge Organization System–Extension for Labels. An ontology for denoting taxonomic relations between entities, with support for rich statements about their labels. https://www.w3.org/TR/skos-reference/skos-xl.html (published 18th of August 2009, last Accessed 3rd of April 2023).

[4] PoolParty Semantic Suite https://www.poolparty.biz/ (last accessed 3rd of April, 2023).

[5] https://huggingface.co/fhswf/bert_de_ner.

[6] https://github.com/stefan-it/fine-tuned-berts-seq.

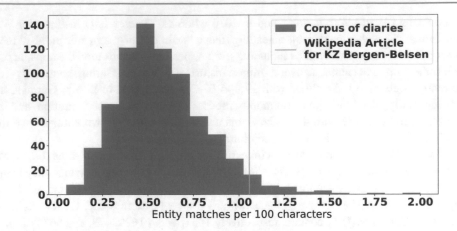

Fig. 1 **Histogram of entity matches per 100 characters, using the WW2 thesaurus.** The corpus was partitioned into overlapping windows of 1000 characters, and the number of entity matches in each was noted

Table 1 **Prevalence of entities from different concept schemes.** Shown are the number of concept matches found for every concept scheme, and in parenthesis, the number of distinct entities in said concept scheme found in each document. Note that the NIOD WW2 Thesaurus is a multi-hierarchy, so a given concept can belong to more than one concept scheme

Document	Internment camps	Organizations	Events	Concepts	Total
Diary 1	134 (13)	18 (7)	37 (10)	1429 (211)	**1618**
Diary 2	12 (2)	3 (2)	7 (2)	566 (116)	**588**
Diary 3	107 (11)	77 (6)	2 (2)	1807 (163)	**1993**
Diary 4	33 (7)	8 (3)	10 (3)	482 (115)	**533**
Diary 5	47 (7)	30 (3)	22 (7)	983 (146)	**1082**
Diary 6	32 (6)	0 (0)	43 (10)	3106 (221)	**3181**
Whole corpus	365 (20)	136 (12)	121 (19)	8373 (405)	

4.1 Entity Extraction

Entity extraction of the six diaries resulted in a total of 8428 concept matches. Given the corpus size, this corresponds to approximately 0.57 concept matches per 100 characters. We contrast this to the German-language Wikipedia article on Bergen-Belsen concentration camp,[7] which exhibits around 1.056 concept matches per 100 characters. See Fig. 1 for a comparison.

The concept matches were distributed among different concept schemes as seen in Table 1, with the most frequently mentioned entities of each shown in Table 2. In general, we see great overlap in the entities mentioned by the different authors.

4.2 Named Entity Recognition

Executing the Named Entity Recognition method on the corpus resulted in a total of 7217 occurrences of 2486 different named entities. These were distributed across entity types as shown in Table 3. Some of these were recognised as entities of different types, so that there were a total of 2355 different strings associated to a named entity.

---

[7] https://de.wikipedia.org/wiki/KZ_Bergen-Belsen last accessed 10th of February 2023.

Table 2 Most common concepts per concept scheme. Places are not shown since in the thesaurus these have only Dutch labels

Organisations	Concepts	Events	Internment camps
Durchgangslager Westerbork	Ostern	Warschauer Aufstand	Lieben
Trawniki	Weihnachten	Beschusse	Vittel
Jewish Agency for	General- gouvernement	Ostfront	Ku
Palestine	Tauschhandel	Schlacht	Grünberg
Sonderkommando	Desinfektion	Abmarsch	Fossoli
SS	Entlausung	Offens	Theresienstadt
American Jewish Joint	Hygiene	Luftkrieg	Drancy
Distribution Committee	Täter	Luftangriff	Durchgangslager
World Jewish Congress	Nachschub	Landungen	Westerbork
Waffen-SS	Hunde	Invasion	Dachau
Rex	Helfer	Machtübernahme	Oranienburg
Reichssicherheitshauptamt	Ghetto	Luftschutzkeller	Treblinka
Luftwaffe	Arbeitslager	Attentat	Sachsenhausen
Germanen	Kapo	Abwerfen	Poniatowa
		Abzug	Neuengamme

Table 3 Distribution of different types of entities in corpus documents

Document	LOC	ORG	OTH	PER	Total
Diary 1	280	105	141	429	**955**
Diary 2	45	3	4	22	**74**
Diary 3	152	28	32	169	**381**
Diary 4	93	11	14	217	**335**
Diary 5	192	21	17	63	**293**
Diary 6	245	16	23	598	**882**
Whole corpus	688	166	213	1419	2486

Table 4 Intersection between concept schemes and entity types

	LOC	ORG	OTH	PER
Concepts	19	3	6	6
Internment camps	18	0	1	3
Organisations	2	3	0	1
Events	0	0	0	0

4.3 Contrasts Between the Results of Both Methods

Of the 2355 different strings that correspond to named entities in the corpus, 45 were also recognised, by the entity extraction tool, as surface forms of an entity in the thesaurus. These 45 entities make up a total of 390 occurrences, and their classification according to named entity type and concept scheme is shown in Table 4. Given that the thesaurus has no concept scheme corresponding to people, any named entities recognised as class PER are errors of the NER tool. A close inspection reveals that, for example, the strings *Brande, Poniatowa* and *Drancy*, which are names of internment camps, are wrongly labelled as people. While such false positives from NER methods are known to happen, previous evaluations of the method used [10] suggest that at least 70% of recognised named entities are correct matches. Identifying the issues that arise in a particular corpus can help fine tune the method or post-process its results.

5 Conclusion and Next Steps

In this exploratory analysis, we used a thesaurus developed to describe a given historical period (WW2 and the Holocaust), to examine first-hand accounts of events from that time. We show that this thesaurus, which has been successfully used for cataloguing historical materials and is well suited for analysing historiographic texts, is less effective for describing texts narrating personal experiences. As evidence supporting this statement, consider the case of the 166 organisations that the NER method has detected in the corpus. Although the thesaurus has a concept scheme containing 1431 organisations, it only contains 3 out of those 166.

We believe this discrepancy exposes the need for augmenting formalised knowledge sources in order to treat documents of a more personal nature. The results also highlight the role that Named Entity Recognition can play in this augmentation process. However, it must be noted that NER results must always be curated by experts when used to enlarge a knowledge organization system (e.g., a thesaurus). This becomes clear in this work, as inspecting the results reveals that several demonyms are detected as locations.

In the next steps, we will create a knowledge graph that brings together the results of NER, the expert-curated vocabularies such as the one used here, and the large collections of entities from bibliographic authority controls and the linked open data cloud.[8]

Acknowledgements The work presented here is part of project MEMORISE. This project is funded by the European Union's Horizon Europe research and innovation programme under grant agreement No. 101061016.

References

1. Benikova, D., Biemann, C., Reznicek, M.: Nosta-d named entity annotation for german: Guidelines and dataset. In: Proceedings of the Ninth International Conference on Language Resources and Evaluation (LREC'14), pp. 2524–2531. European Language Resources Association (ELRA), Reykjavik, Iceland (2014)
2. Edelstein, D., Findlen, P., Ceserani, G., Winterer, C., Coleman, N.: Historical research in a digital age: Reflections from the mapping the republic of letters project. Am. Hist. Rev. **122**(2), 400–424 (2017)
3. Hubková, H., Kral, P.: Transfer learning for Czech historical named entity recognition. In: Proceedings of the International Conference on Recent Advances in Natural Language Processing (RANLP 2021), pp. 576–582. INCOMA Ltd., Held Online (2021)
4. Humbel, M., Nyhan, J., Vlachidis, A., Kim, S., Ortolja, A.: Named entity recognition for early-modern textual sources: a review of capabilities and challenges with strategies for the future. J. Document. **6** (2021)
5. Hyvönen, E.: "sampo" model and semantic portals for digital humanities on the semantic web. In: Proceedings of the Digital Humanities in the Nordic Countries 5th Conference (DHN 2020). CEUR-WS.org (2020)
6. Jänicke, S., Franzini, G., Cheema, M.F., Scheuermann, G.: Visual text analysis in digital humanities. In: Computer Graphics Forum, vol. 36, pp. 226–250. Wiley Online Library (2017)
7. Khulusi, R., Billib, S., Jänicke, S.: Exploring life in concentration camps through a visual analysis of prisoners' diaries. Information **13**(2) (2022)
8. Krabina, B.: Building a knowledge graph for the history of vienna with semantic mediawiki. J. Web Semant. **76**, 100771 (2023)
9. Kusnick, J., Andersen, N.S., Beck, S., Doppler, C., Koch, S., Liem, J., Mayr, E., Seirafi, K., Windhager, F., Jänicke, S.: A survey on visualization-based storytelling in digital humanities. In: Computer Graphics Forum. Wiley Online Library (2023) (in review)
10. Labusch, K., Kulturbesitz, P., Neudecker, C., Zellhöfer, D.: Bert for named entity recognition in contemporary and historical german. In: Proceedings of the 15th Conference on Natural Language Processing, pp. 8–11. Erlangen, Germany (2019)
11. Nandwani, P., Verma, R.: A review on sentiment analysis and emotion detection from text. Soc. Network Anal. Min. **11**(1), 81 (2021)
12. van Nispen, A., Jongma, L.: Holocaust and world war two linked open data developments in the netherlands. Umanistica Digitale **4** (2019)
13. Psutka, J., Švec, J., Psutka, J.V., Vaněk, J., Pražák, A., Ircing, P.: System for fast lexical and phonetic spoken term detection in a czech cultural heritage archive. EURASIP J. Audio Speech Music Process. 1–11 (2011)
14. Rovera, M., Nanni, F., Ponzetto, S., Goy, A.: Domain-specific Named Entity Disambiguation in Historical Memoirs, pp. 287–291 (2017)
15. Schweter, S., März, L., Schmid, K., Çano, E.: hmbert: Historical multilingual language models for named entity recognition. In: Faggioli, G., Ferro, N., Hanbury, A., Potthast, M. (eds.) Proceedings of the Working Notes of CLEF 2022–Conference and Labs of the Evaluation Forum, Bologna, Italy, September 5th–to–8th, 2022. CEUR Workshop Proceedings, vol. 3180, pp. 1109–1129. CEUR-WS.org (2022)
16. Segel, E., Heer, J.: Narrative visualization: Telling stories with data. IEEE Trans. Vis. Comput. Graph. **16**(6), 1139–1148 (2010)
17. Vassilakis, C., Kotis, K., Spiliotopoulos, D., Margaris, D., Kasapakis, V., Anagnostopoulos, C.N., Santipantakis, G., Vouros, G.A., Kotsilieris, T., Petukhova, V., Malchanau, A., Lykourentzou, I., Helin, K.M., Revenko, A., Gligoric, N., Pokric, B.: A semantic mixed reality framework for shared cultural experiences ecosystems. Big Data Cogn. Comput. **4**(2) (2020)
18. Windhager, F., Federico, P., Schreder, G., Glinka, K., Dörk, M., Miksch, S., Mayr, E.: Visualization of cultural heritage collection data: state of the art and future challenges. IEEE Trans. Vis. Comput. Graph. **25**(6), 2311–2330 (2018)

---

[8] https://memorise.sdu.dk/.

Applications and Use Cases

Supply Chain Data Spaces–The Next Generation of Data Sharing

Angela Fessl, Gert Breitfuß, Nina Popanton, Julia Pichler, Carina Hochstrasser, Michael Plasch, and Michael Herburger

Abstract The economy is heavily dependent on closely coordinated and optimised supply chain processes with an increased demand for data sharing and supply chain visibility. Industrial supply chain data spaces offer a way to deal with this demand. In this work, we present three business cases from different domains – steel industry, food industry, and manufacturing industry – derived from a workshop series with stakeholders from Austrian industries that will contribute significantly to the development of an Austrian supply chain data space concept.

Keywords Supply chain data spaces · Data sharing · Business case

1 Introduction

The ongoing digitisation causes a shift from the traditional interpretation of supply chains as static systems towards complex adaptive systems as conditions like the availability of natural resources cannot be seen as stable anymore [1]. Data is seen as the "oil of the digital age", replacing oil as the most valuable resource [2]. As a result, data is ubiquitous, supporting companies and supply chains in their daily operations and providing essential input for decisions at all company levels. This data-driven decision-making basis is essential for industrial supply chains. Tightly coordinated and optimised supply chain processes require a high degree of flexibility and inter-organisational data exchange and visibility in the supply chain, ideally end-to-end, from consumer to raw material. This ambition can be supported by industrial supply chain data spaces, similar to the European initiatives Gaia-X [3] or the International Data Space Association (IDSA) [4] who are working towards shared infrastructures and common European data spaces to create a European data ecosystem. In this work we present first insights from a workshop series about how a supply chain data space for Austrian industries could look like.

2 Supply Chain Data Space for Austrian Industries

Our work is based on the Smart Connected Supplier Network (SCSN), which is best practice example for exchanging information in the supply chain that allows small and medium enterprises (SMEs) to share data more easily, quickly and reliably. Inspired by the SCSN, data spaces build the stakeholder platform for relevant actors (data providers, data consumers, service providers and intermediaries) to securely share and access data assets as depicted in Fig. 1. Thus, to be able to develop a successful industrial supply chain data space for Austria, the following design characteristics need to be considered:

A. Fessl · G. Breitfuß
Know-Center GmbH, Sandgasse 36, 8010 Graz, Austria
e-mail: breitfuss@know-center.at

A. Fessl (✉)
Graz University of Technology, Sandgasse 36, 8010 Graz, Austria
e-mail: afessl@know-center.at

N. Popanton
Data Intelligence Offensive, Thurngasse 8/12, 1090 Wien, Austria

J. Pichler · C. Hochstrasser · M. Plasch · M. Herburger
University of Applied Sciences Upper Austria, Campus Steyr, Logistikum, Wehrgrabengasse 1–3, 4400 Steyr, Austria

© The Author(s), under exclusive license to Springer Nature Switzerland AG 2024
P. Haber et al. (eds.), *Data Science—Analytics and Applications*,
https://doi.org/10.1007/978-3-031-42171-6_11

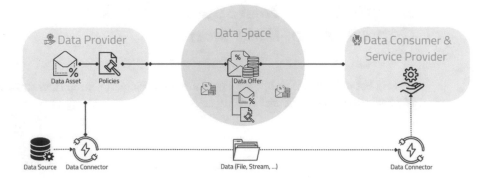

Fig. 1 Presentation of a supply chain data space - Copyright notice: ©Data Intelligence Offensive (DIO)

- **Decentral by design**: the data space needs to consist of a decentralised and distributed data infrastructure on which novel business cases can be built upon. This design characteristics prevents the development of an other cloud system where all data is stored and ensures the data sovereignty of the data providers.
- **Sovereignty and security by design**: Data providers only need to describe their data using metadata. They keep their data in-house, thus, maintaining the data sovereignty and ensuring the greatest possible control over one's own data. For exchanging the data, individual contracts between the data consumers and the data providers need to be set up.
- **Domain specific design**: Depending on the domain, data spaces need to fulfil specific requirements and need of the domain, however, the federation with other domain specific data spaces need to be established.
- **Simplicity by design**: 1:n linking is implemented–being connected once, reduces the effort to exchange data with the entire supply chain data space community.

To develop a concrete concept of an industrial supply chain data space, we have conducted a workshop series to derive relevant business cases.

3 Methodology

Four subsequent 3-hours workshops were conducted in Austria (Vienna, Linz, Graz, Online). Five to ten stakeholders with respective supply chain knowledge of their domain participated in each workshop. Each workshop followed the same procedure: (i) introduction to the workshop and the related project, (ii) group discussion 1: actual state of data sharing practices, (iii) introduction to the data space concept; and (iv) group discussion 2: new business cases enabled by data space.

4 Results

From the workshop series, we derived the following three business cases that will serve as a baseline to develop an Austrian data space concept:

Business Case 1: Steel industry: A big steel producing company is manufacturing oil drills for drilling rigs. This company is selling the oil drills to a company that is delivering them to drilling rigs all over the world e.g., Asia, Africa or Europe. As the lifetime of a steel drill is limited, at some point in time the oil drills need to be replaced and the old steel drills are scrapped. For the steel producing company it would be of great interest to know, when their originally created steel drills are scrapped, whom to contact to re-buy the steel, and whom to involve to bring back the steel to Austria to manufacture new steel products. A domain specific data space, where the steel producing company could exchange data about their manufactured steel drills would help to solve this problem.

Business Case 2: Food industry: The Austrian law stipulates that when meat is sold in a supermarket, the whole supply chain including all involved stakeholders need to have all information about the meat in a traceable, transparent and reproducible way. This supply chain starts with the cow born and growing up on a farm, goes over to the slaughterhouse, and includes all suppliers bringing the meat from one place to another. Thus, a supply chain data space where all relevant players are enrolled and all information about the meat and its handling process could be exchanged would significantly facilitate the prescribed tracking process.

Business Case 3: Manufacturing Industry: Manufacturing companies often face challenges in obtaining current data and information from suppliers, due to the diversity of supplier sizes and sectors. Currently, the exchange of data is limited to order information between the manufacturing company and large suppliers through e.g., EDI (Electronic Data Interchange) connections. The data exchange with smaller or larger suppliers is unstructured, irregular, and conducted through various communication channels. A uniform, scalable, and easy-to-use data exchange model can be achieved through a data space that accommodates both small and large companies and integrates along the entire supply chain.

5 Conclusion and Outlook

By identifying and concretising business cases from the Austrian industries, we see high potential and relevance for developing a supply chain data space for Austria. In a next step, we will derive a general concept for a data space that will be elaborated and validated in relation to one or two of our business cases and that will then serve as a blueprint for a concrete implementation.

Acknowledgements Know-Center is a COMET Center within the COMET–Competence Centers for Excellent Technologies Programme and funded by BMK, BMAW as well as the co-financing provinces Styria, Vienna and Tyrol. COMET is managed by FFG. The "dataSChare" project is funded as part of the ICT of the future research program by the FFG. The funding of the project "dataSChare" as part of the ICT of the future research program enabled the cross-domain research in the field of data spaces.

References

1. Wieland, A.: Dancing the supply chain: Toward transformative supply chain management. J. Supply Chain Manag. **57**(1), 58–73 (2021)
2. Forbes Homepage: https://www.forbes.com/sites/perryrotella/2012/04/02/is-data-the-new-oil/?sh=4c4c02f97db3. Last accessed 20 Jan 2023
3. GAIA-X: https://www.gaia-x.eu/. Last accessed 20 Jan 2023
4. IDSA: https://internationaldataspaces.org/. Last accessed 20 Jan 2023
5. Smart Connected Supplier Network (SCSN): https://smart-connected.nl. Last accessed 23 Mar 2023

Condition Monitoring and Anomaly Detection: Real-World Challenges and Successes

Katharina Dimovski, Léo Bonal, Thomas Zengerle, Ulrich Hüttinger, Norbert Linder, and Doris Entner

Abstract Data science projects in industry come with many challenges – from idea exploration over proof-of-concept implementation to deployment. This paper shows along the use case of detecting anomalies in LED drivers how to successfully approach such a project. Focus is put on the anomaly detection using machine learning methods, namely one-class SVMs, isolation forests, and LSTM-based autoencoders. The algorithms show promising results; all detected anomalies can be linked to an abnormality in the data. These anomalies will be analysed by domain experts to optimize the product design and the production process. Furthermore, the successful proof-of-concept implementation justifies the investment into a global deployment of the anomaly detection in other development and production sites.

Keywords Condition monitoring · Digital twin · Anomaly detection

1 Introduction

This paper presents a data science project in industry and highlights the changing challenges along the project phases from idea and data exploration over the proof of concept (PoC) implementation to the solution's deployment. The targeted product is a LED driver deployed in millions of luminaires globally. The goal is to acquire insights into the usage and condition of driver components along their life-cycle. Machine learning (ML) methods are applied to detect anomalies in the collected driver data, linking them to environmental conditions and failure modes. Overall, the expected benefits are product and production optimization, cost reductions and novel product features. To achieve these benefits, the project is divided into three phases as shown in Fig. 1. The first phase mainly focused on collecting ideas and exploring data. An initial use case was the prediction of the LED driver lifespan. However, the available data, based on customer feedback regarding failures and the end of life, were scarce and non-representative. Thus, the quality of the predictions was challenging to evaluate and generalize. Even though this first phase did not generate an immediate benefit, the gained insights led to clearly defined actions for the follow-up proof of concept (PoC) phase. A use case was defined for the systematic collection of driver data in controlled environments, with the aim of detecting anomalies. The used methodology and methods, the results and discussion, as well as the conclusion of the PoC and the (ongoing) deployment phases are detailed in the following sections.

2 Methodology

Data science projects in industry often follow the Cross Industry Standard Process for Data Mining (CRISP-DM, [1]). It consists of six steps: business understanding, data understanding, data preparation, modeling, evaluation, and deployment, each detailed below.

The business and data understanding go hand in hand. The defined use case was to detect non-normal behaviour of the driver along the life-cycle in controlled test environments, particularly in a highly accelerated stress screening (HASS) chamber

K. Dimovski (✉) · L. Bonal · D. Entner
V-Research GmbH, Stadtstraße 33, 6850 Dornbirn, Austria
e-mail: katharina.dimovski@v-research.at

T. Zengerle · U. Hüttinger · N. Linder
Tridonic GmbH & Co G, Färbergasse 15, 6851 Dornbirn, Austria

© The Author(s), under exclusive license to Springer Nature Switzerland AG 2024
P. Haber et al. (eds.), *Data Science—Analytics and Applications*,
https://doi.org/10.1007/978-3-031-42171-6_12

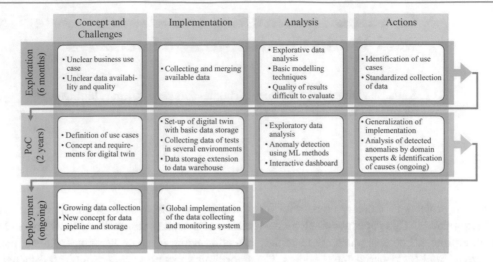

Fig. 1 The concepts and challenges, implementation, analysis, and actions of the project divided into the three development phases exploration, PoC and deployment

and a humidity chamber. This is expected to provide further insights in the driver's actual condition and remaining lifespan. Simultaneously, the digital twin [2] for a systematic data collection in the chamber and data storage was conceptualized, set up, and embedded in the existing IT infrastructure. In each chamber, 15 drivers are tested under extreme, cyclic stress conditions. For both experimental settings, around 20 features were recorded roughly every 10 s over a period of three months with a cycle length of three hours. A thorough exploratory data analysis was carried out and first visualizations were made to inspect the data. The implementation was done in Python [4].

The data were prepared for modeling by normalizing them to zero mean and unit variance, filling in missing values with the nearest value if the time period was shorter than 30 minutes, and excluding them otherwise. Based on expert knowledge and exploratory data analysis, eight features were selected from the recorded data. A sliding window approach with a window length of six hours was used to split the time series data into samples while still capturing temporal dependencies in the data. The resulting samples were divided into training and test sets, where the training set encompassed the first month of data collection. This measure was put in place to ensure, backed by visual inspection, that the data do not contain anomalies associated with product failure but only a few point anomalies related to a temporary malfunction of the test setup. The train-test-split of the data as well as a point anomaly in the training data (longer cycle) are shown in Fig. 2.

In the modeling stage of CRISP-DM, anomalies were detected using different ML-methods, specifically one-class support vector machines (SVMs), isolation forests, and long-short-term-memory (LSTM) based autoencoders, as described in [3]. The hyperparameters for these algorithms were selected using a combination of trial and error as well as visual inspection of the results.

For the evaluation step, the algorithms return an anomaly score. For one-class SVMs, it is based on the distance to the classification boundary, while isolation forests calculate the score based on the depth of the decision tree used to separate a sample. In the case of LSTM-based autoencoders, the mean-squared error (MSE) between the input and output is employed. To establish a baseline, data without anomalies are used, which is valid since the settings of the HASS and humidity chamber remained stable throughout the data collection. In this way, if a sample's score deviates from the baseline, an anomaly can be expected. Furthermore, visual inspection of the data is used to verify the detected anomalies.

The deployment phase (ongoing) requires a generalization of the PoC implementation, including the use of a validation data set. A thorough comparison of suitable database solutions, code refactoring and modularization are used to prepare the data pipeline, storage concept and algorithms for the global deployment of anomaly detection and integration of new/adapted models in other development and production sites.

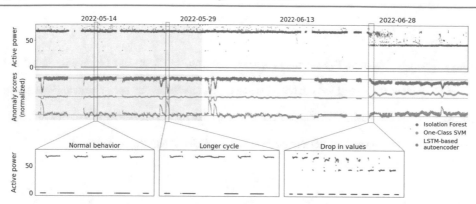

Fig. 2 The top graph shows measured data for the feature "active power" from the HASS chamber. The grey background indicates training samples, and the remaining data are test samples. The middle graph shows the algorithms' normalized anomaly scores. The baseline for normal samples is marked by a horizontal line. The bottom row displays data for normal behavior, a too long cycle, and one value drop

3 Results and Discussion

To visualize the data and results of the algorithms, a dashboard was created. Even though visual inspection of the data is cumbersome, a few anomalies were found manually, which were also detected using the ML-algorithms. In total, the algorithms detected about 40 anomalies in the data, all of which could be clearly linked to an abnormality in some of the features. For example, as shown in Fig. 2, changes in active power were accompanied by changes in the magnitude and pattern of the anomaly scores. An initial analysis by domain experts revealed that the anomalies had varying causes, such as errors in the HASS chamber (e.g., longer cycles) or data collection (e.g., zero values for certain variables), and device failures (e.g., drop or drift in power).

The classical ML methods, namely one-class SVM and isolation forest, were not originally intended for temporal data analysis, in contrast to LSTM-based autoencoders which were specifically designed for this purpose. Nonetheless, it is noteworthy that all methods demonstrate comparable performance. Further performance improvement is anticipated through systematic tuning of the hyperparameters. Moreover, it is recommended to assess the performance of all approaches on additional data sets, such as driver data from real-world, uncontrolled environments.

The third phase of the project focuses on the global deployment of the anomaly detection. Besides the generalized data pipeline and collection, a special focus is put on the integration of modular software components to facilitate the seamless incorporation of adapted or new models. Moreover, the PoC-phase has also revealed opportunities for further research and development. To turn the detected anomalies into knowledge and actions, domain experts will classify them to (automatically) judge whether the product is failing or needs replacement/repair. Additionally, the resulting insights from the anomaly detection will be shared with engineers to optimize product design and improve the production process.

4 Conclusion

The project resulted in a digital twin software, persistent data storage design, PoC for anomaly detection and an interactive dashboard for data and results visualization. It paved the way for the vision of deploying the digital twin and the anomaly detection globally. Keys to success were the close collaboration between data science experts and the domain experts as well as the freedom to explore possibilities and potentials in the starting phase without generating an immediate benefit. This yielded a well-founded use case definition and concept for establishing the digital twin.

Acknowledgements This work was carried out within the "Basisprogramm" funded by the Austrian Research Promotion Agency (FFG).

References

1. Chapman, P., Clinton, J., Kerber, R., Khabaza, T., Reinartz, T., Shearer, C., Wirth, R.: CRSIP-DM 1.0: Step-by-Step Data Mining Guide. SPSS Inc (2000)
2. Fuller, A., Fan, Z., Day, C., Barlow, C.: Digital twin: Enabling technologies, challenges and open research. IEEE Access **8**, 108952–108971 (2020)
3. Nassif, A.B., Talib, M.A., Nasir, Q., Dakalbab, F.M.: Machine learning for anomaly detection: A systematic review. IEEE Access **9**, 78658–78700 (2021)
4. Python Software Foundation: Python Language Reference (version 3.9). Available at http://www.python.org

Towards Validated Head Tracking On Moving Two-Wheelers

Wolfgang Kremser, Sebastian Mayr, Simon Lassl, Marco Holzer, and Martin Tiefengrabner

Abstract We investigate the problem of validating head tracking methods while riding two-wheelers. A low-cost inertial measurement unit and an image-based system using fiducial markers are compared against a wearable motion capture system. Results show that both systems are capable of tracking head motion. However, signal drift correction and hardening against outdoor conditions are required to make the systems viable in real-life use.

Keywords IMU · Head tracking · Motion capture · Fiducial markers

1 Introduction

Knowing head movements while riding two-wheelers is key to understanding the interaction between vehicle and rider. These movements can be digitized using inertial measurement units (IMUs). A preliminary feasibility study used two low-cost IMUs (Movesense Active, Movesense Ltd.) attached to the vehicle and head, and the Madgwick algorithm [2] for head tracking.

The results lacked rigorous validation though. A literature research using the SCOPUS and Web of Science databases could not produce a study design for validating head tracking while riding a two-wheeler. This work is a step towards such a study design. We build upon the results of the feasibility study by re-evaluating its results using a wearable motion capture system. Furthermore, we present an image-based alternative to IMU-based head tracking.

2 Methods

Data was collected at various speeds on a closed test track with a figure-eight shape. In addition to the aforementioned Movesense setup, the test rider wore the XSens Awinda (Movella Inc.) IMU-based motion capture system, which acted as the reference system, under their protective gear. Another IMU attached to the two-wheeler's frame was used to estimate the vehicle's lean angle. Furthermore, a helmet-mounted GoPro Hero 10 filmed a board with printed ArUco markers [1] at 30 frames per second. The board was mounted on the vehicle's frame at the base of the handlebars. Each system was calibrated according to their recommended procedure, and their clocks were synchronized using Network Time Protocol (NTP), a continuous Longitudinal Timecode (LTC) signal, and, in post-processing, cross-correlation.

For data analysis, each output was down-sampled to 30Hz and segmented into four different curve types ('left' or 'right', and 'long' or 'short') based on the bike's lean angle. For each curve, for both the Movesense and ArUco method, the root mean square error (RMSE) of the Euler angles with respect to the Awinda reference was computed. A spline regression between RMSE and time was applied to identify any drift.

W. Kremser (✉) · S. Mayr
Salzburg Research Forschungsgesellschaft mbH, Salzburg, Austria
e-mail: wolfgang.kremser@salzburgresearch.at

S. Lassl · M. Holzer
Biwak Outdoor & Research OG, Vienna, Austria

M. Tiefengrabner
Pierer Innovation GmbH, Wels, Austria

© The Author(s), under exclusive license to Springer Nature Switzerland AG 2024
P. Haber et al. (eds.), *Data Science—Analytics and Applications*,
https://doi.org/10.1007/978-3-031-42171-6_13

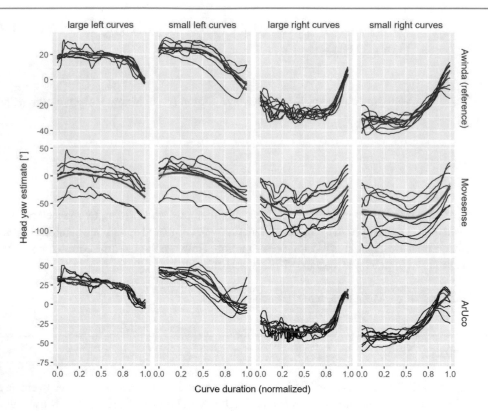

Fig. 1 Overview of all analyzed left and right curves, with the mean curve in red

Table 1 Mean, standard deviation, minimum and maximum of the yaw's RMSE

Yaw angle RMSE (°)	μ	σ	min	max
Movesense (curves before drift)	11.92	3.0	7.5	18.1
Movesense (all curves)	33.2	23.5	0.54	82.6
ArUco	9.3	5.9	0.2	30.9

3   Results

65 curve segments were analyzed. They are summarized in Fig. 1. We focused on the head's yaw angle, as it determines the forward direction.

Table 1 shows the RMSE staticstics. The spline regression (Fig. 2) revealed that after 120 s, Movesense's yaw estimate starts to drift noticeably. Since the ArUco method works on a frame-by-frame basis, there is no time dependency between frames and thus, no drift. However, the yaw estimate contained artifacts (see Fig. 3). Reviewing the video footage, we noticed that in these cases, the algorithm mistook some other geometry in the frame (e.g., a screw on the two-wheeler or shadow from overhead tree foliage) as the marker.

4   Discussion and Conclusion

Before the drift onset, both Movesense and ArUco have similar accuracy regarding head yaw angle estimation. With proper drift correction for Movesense, and more robust marker tracking and outlier handling for ArUco, both systems may be cost-effective methods for head tracking applications on moving two-wheelers.

There are open questions regarding Awinda's validity when used on moving two-wheelers. Although the system is widely used in sports and exercise research, its validity in this scenario is not yet fully understood. Vibrations from the vehicle, road surface conditions, and the displacement by the protective gear worn over the sensors may affect the accuracy of the motion

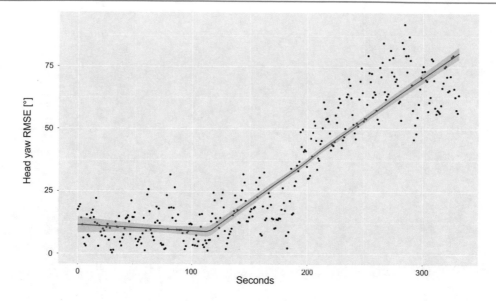

Fig. 2 Linear spline regression (blue) of RMSE between Awinda and Movesense with 95% confidence interval (grey area). The two individual regression lines have a slope of $-0.023°$/s and $0.333°$/s respectively

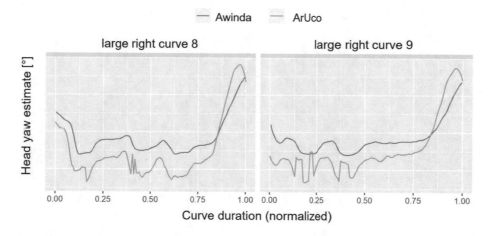

Fig. 3 Comparison between Awinda and ArUco on large right curves number 8 and number 9. Curve 8 shows short-term artifacts that last a single frame, whereas curve 9 contains artifacts that last multiple frames

tracking. This limits its usefulness for the purpose of validating other systems in this environment. In this study, Awinda's output was plausible and free from drift and artifacts. However, future research should integrate external equipment (e.g., LIDAR sensors, marker-based motion tracking) to rigorously determine Awinda's validity on moving two-wheelers.

Acknowledgements Details regarding vehicle type were omitted to protect intellectual property. Funded by the Austrian Research Promotion Agency in project #895244.

References

1. Garrido-Jurado, S., Muñoz-Salinas, R., Madrid-Cuevas, F.J., Marín-Jiménez, M.J.: Automatic generation and detection of highly reliable fiducial markers under occlusion. Pattern Recognit. **47**(6), 2280–2292 (2014)
2. Madgwick, S.O.H., Harrison, A.J.L., Vaidyanathan, R.: Estimation of IMU and MARG orientation using a gradient descent algorithm. IEEE Int. Conf. Rehabil. Robot. **2011**, 1–7 (2011)

A Framework for Inline Quality Inspection of Mechanical Components in an Industrial Production

Reduction of Development Time and Increase of Classification Performance by Using a Data-Centric Deep Learning Approach

Christian Prechtl, Sebastian Bomberg, and Florian Jungreithmaier

Abstract Automated quality inspection of components in industrial production environments is one of the main requirements to achieve current productivity and quality goals. Since conventional inspection systems have only partially met these requirements, and research projects in the industry have hardly been practicable in this area, MIBA AG has developed a quality inspection framework of its high-quality components to achieve these goals in its production facilities. Using deep learning and focusing on the data-centric approach are the key success factors of those quality inspection systems. This technical report describes the developed framework, and the results are discussed.

Keywords Quality Inspection · Deep Learning · Data Centric · Computer Vision

1 Introduction

MIBA AG is a technology group that produces electronic components, powder metal parts, friction material, and plain bearings in large quantities, among other things. A framework for classifying good and faulty components has been developed in recent years to inspect these components automatically in the production line.

Keeping development times short and reacting quickly to changes was a major requirement. It is important to adapt the detection accordingly, especially when production conditions change, without overlooking defective components and keeping the misclassification of defect-free components as low as possible. Furthermore, the near real-time inference of the component inspection is critical to ensure high productivity.

To keep the framework as lean as possible, MATLAB was used as a single development environment without losing the ability to integrate other Software components. For the implementation of the applications, it was of great importance that MATLAB provides several toolboxes and tools in industrial quality. As a company, MathWorks is a sustainable partner in the field of image processing and machine learning.

Using machine learning methods (e.g., deep learning) led to meeting the classification performance requirements metrics such as True Positive, False Positive, True Negative, and False Negative rates. As advocated in current research, developing deep learning models is based on the data-centric approach [4].

C. Prechtl (✉)
MIBA AG, Dr.-Mitterbauer-Straße 3, 4663 Laakirchen, Austria
e-mail: christian.prechtl@miba.com

S. Bomberg
The MathWorks GmbH, Weihenstephaner Str. 6, 81637 Munich, Germany

F. Jungreithmaier
MIBA Sinter Austria GmbH, Dr.-Mitterbauer-Straße 1, 4655 Vorchdorf, Austria

© The Author(s), under exclusive license to Springer Nature Switzerland AG 2024
P. Haber et al. (eds.), *Data Science—Analytics and Applications*,
https://doi.org/10.1007/978-3-031-42171-6_14

2 State of the Art

Rules-based machine vision systems may produce a high rejection rate in specific scenarios. Follow-up inspections are to be expected when there is variation in the parts or in the environment the system operates in, such as time-varying lighting conditions. Adapting rules to new parts may require several iterations and delay the use of the system in production. Deep learning models (i.e., neural networks) learn from data to perform tasks on images, such as anomaly detection [1], classification, and object detection [2, 3]. These models learn their own rules that may be automatically adapted to new conditions as more data becomes available. Since the 2010s, deep neural networks involving millions of parameters have been trained on large datasets. Model accuracy was then improved by iterating on the model architecture, hyper-parameters, and training algorithms.

In 2022, Andrew Ng proposed a data-centric approach to AI and deep learning: Instead of optimizing the model, developers should leverage pre-trained network transfer learning and focus on carefully selecting and processing training data [4]. This is especially true for applications, such as optical inspection, where little data is available and biased towards a majority class (e.g., non-defects). Accuracy can improve, and this approach can shorten development cycles significantly.

3 Quality Inspection Framework

The quality inspection framework described in this paper includes both hardware components and software modules. Figure 1 shows the framework with individual modules. The modules are packaged with MATLAB Compiler into applications deployed on an industrial PC directly at the quality inspection system. The applications can be updated and redeployed quickly at no additional cost. Neural networks and parameter files can be replaced at runtime.

Hardware Setup. Selecting the appropriate hardware is crucial in the first '*Data & Image Acquisition*' module for data or image acquisition. The hardware was selected based on the defect sizes, defect appearance, and environmental conditions.

Software Setup. Basic image processing methods were developed and integrated into the '*Preprocessing*' module to prepare the raw image for the '*Classification & Reasoning*' module.

The '*Classification & Reasoning*' and '*Data-Centric Model Training*' modules are used to train and integrate deep learning models into the quality inspection framework. In developing these two modules, we focused on providing quick updates and automated training and testing steps with the goal to keep the '*Model customization cycle*' as efficient as possible during execution and production. This enables the developer to adapt the deep learning model, validate, and put it back into production in the event of new data or reduced performance in less than an hour.

The '*Communication*' module provides communication to controllers (PLC), human machine interfaces (HMI), and databases.

Data-Centric Approach. Instead of iterating on the network topology and training parameters selection, the framework provides a software tool to automatically train multiple networks in parallel and select the best model and parameters. The focus is directed at identifying mislabeled and underrepresented data. The convolutional neural networks (CNN) were mostly trained from scratch. The networks are about 15–21 layers in size. The input neurons correspond to image dimensions and channels, and the neurons in the output layer represent the classes (Fig. 2).

Fig. 1 Illustration of the quality inspection framework and description of the individual software modules. The core of the modules is the 'model customization cycle'

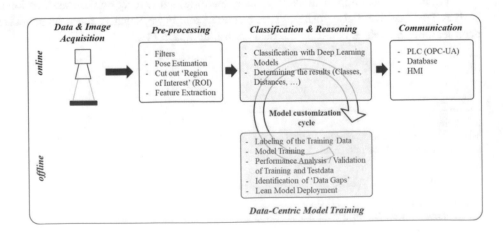

Fig. 2 Training data set examples of binary and multiclass classification problems

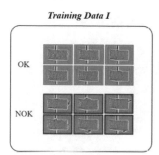

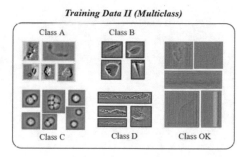

4 Results and Discussion

The framework described in this report has been developed over the last four years. In the first year alone, the increased use of deep learning and the data-centric approach led to the rollout of more inspection systems than in the previous five years combined.

In addition to the development of standardized hardware solutions in the years 2020 and 2021, the described framework was further developed on the software side and supplemented with corresponding user-friendly tools (e.g., for automated training, testing, validation of the neural networks, and applications) for labeling failure-part data and for analyzing current production performance.

Compared to conventional, rules-based inspection systems in our production facilities, we reduced the development time by 30–50%. However, the greatest advantage compared to other systems is the significant reduction of pseudo-rejects and the short network update time. Compared with conventional systems used in the past, we have only 25% of the initial pseudo scrap (4 inspection systems were compared for 6 months, in each case). The described approach leads to an update time of less than one hour for neural networks. Conversely, approving changes for other systems with a comparable amount of data can take more than half a day.

In the last years, the focus was on rolling out these applications, further generalizing the framework, and identifying other use cases in the company. These developments have always been driven by the goal of increasing productivity, keeping failures and downtimes as low as possible, and meeting increasing quality demands. The collected data from the inspection systems are used at MIBA production facilities to improve component quality and detect early-stage defects continuously. Using MATLAB and its open interfaces to hardware and other software as the robust backbone for the framework has proven to be a great strength.

Inspection system design and neural network training still require appropriate education and experience. Further generalizations, automation, and simplifications of the framework are needed to make it usable for a larger group. Going forward, we will continue to increase the performance of the deep learning networks, the framework, and the quality inspection systems. A strong focus will also be on increasing the number of applications and systems and continuously reducing the development time and complexity of those systems.

References

1. Kingma, D. P., Welling M.: Auto-encoding variational Bayes (2013). https://doi.org/10.48550/arXiv.1312.6114
2. Ross, G.: Fast R-CNN. In: Proceedings of the IEEE International Conference on Computer Vision, pp. 1440–1448. IEEE Computer Society, Washington DC (2015)
3. Redmon, J., Divvala, S., Girshick, R., Farhadi, A.: You only look once: unified, real-time object detection. In: 2016 IEEE Conference on Computer Vision and Pattern Recognition (CVPR), pp. 779–788. IEEE Computer Society, Washington DC (2016)
4. Strickland, E.: Andrew Ng, AI minimalist: the machine-learning pioneer says small is the new big. IEEE Spectr. **59**(4), 22–50 (2022)

A Modular Test Bed for Reinforcement Learning Incorporation into Industrial Applications

Reuf Kozlica⬤, Georg Schäfer⬤, Simon Hirländer, and Stefan Wegenkittl⬤

Abstract This application paper explores the potential of using reinforcement learning (RL) to address the demands of Industry 4.0, including shorter time-to-market, mass customization, and batch size one production. Specifically, we present a use case in which the task is to transport and assemble goods through a model factory following predefined rules. Each simulation run involves placing a specific number of goods of random color at the entry point. The objective is to transport the goods to the assembly station, where two rivets are installed in each product, connecting the upper part to the lower part. Following the installation of rivets, blue products must be transported to the exit, while green products are to be transported to storage. The study focuses on the application of reinforcement learning techniques to address this problem and improve the efficiency of the production process.

Keywords Reinforcement learning · Industry 4.0 · OPC UA

1   Introduction

Schäfer et al. stress how Reinforcement Learning (RL) can be used to overcome demands posed by the concepts of Industry 4.0, including shorter time-to-market, mass customization of products, and batch size one production proposing an Operational Technology (OT)-aware RL architecture in [8]. RL is an important machine learning paradigm for Industry 4.0 because it has the potential to surpass human level performance in various complex tasks [6] and does not require pre-generated data in advance. RL agents can learn optimal policies for executing control tasks, potentially leading to productivity maximization and cost reduction [3]. RL agents can also explore their environment to generate new data, which is particularly useful in environments where data is scarce. Additionally, RL agents can exploit their environment to detect unexpected behavior early on, supporting the creation of more realistic digital representations of the environment. For more information on RL refer to Sutton & Barto [9].

Based on a quantitative text analysis and a qualitative literature review, Hermann et al. [2] identified the following four Industry 4.0 design principles, which we are addressing with the created test bed: (i) Decentralized Decisions, (ii) Technical Assistance, (iii) Interconnection and (iv) Information Transparency. (i) and (ii) describe the interconnection of objects and

*Reuf Kozlica and Simon Hirländer are supported by the Lab for Intelligent Data Analytics Salzburg (IDA Lab) funded by Land Salzburg (WISS 2025) under project number 20102-F1901166-KZP. Georg Schäfer is supported by the JRC ISIA project funded by the Christian Doppler Research Association.

R. Kozlica (✉) · G. Schäfer · S. Wegenkittl
Salzburg University of Applied Sciences, Salzburg, Austria
e-mail: reuf.kozlica@fh-salzburg.ac.at

G. Schäfer
e-mail: georg.schaefer@fh-salzburg.ac.at

S. Wegenkittl
e-mail: stefan.wegenkittl@fh-salzburg.ac.at

S. Hirländer
Paris Lodron University Salzburg, Salzburg, Austria
e-mail: simon.hirlaender@plus.ac.at

people which allows for decentralized decision-making in Industry 4.0 enabled by Cyber-Physical Systems (CPSs). Meanwhile, humans' role is shifting towards strategic decision-making and problem-solving, supported by assistance systems and physical support by robots. Including RL into the aforementioned setting allows for incorporation of both principles. (iii) and (iv) address the increasing number of interconnected objects and people in the Internet of Everything (IoE) which enables collaborations and information transparency, but also requires common communication standards and cybersecurity, and relies on context-aware systems for appropriate decision-making based on real-time information provision. Combining Open Platform Communication Unified Architecture (OPC UA) [5] with the standard RL setting, as we are proposing in [8], enables the support for design principles (iii) and (iv).

2 Test Bed

The case study presented by [7] and extended by [1] aims to simulate a real production system using a model factory. The model factory, depicted in Fig. 1, comprises five modules: entry, rotary table, assembly station, storage, and exit. The entry storage of the model factory stores three different types of parts, namely the transport carriage, lower part of the product, and upper part of the product. The transport carriage is used for moving goods on the conveyor belts, while the lower and upper parts of the product are required for product assembly. The rotary table, which serves as a pivotal element in the model factory, can transport goods from the entry to the storage unit or from the entry to the assembly station. At the assembly station, rivets must be added to the product, and during the insertion process, the conveyor must remain stationary. The assembled products come in different randomly assigned colors. The factory is also equipped with several sensors that track the products on their carriages as they move through the facility, and can recognize the color and presence of rivets in a product.[1]

The model is designed to be representative of a real production system and includes several important aspects such as transportation of goods using conveyor belts and a rotary table, product modification through the assembly station, and storage of goods in both entry point and the main storage unit. Moreover, it represents a modular production plant consisting of multiple Programmable Logic Controllers (PLCs) of different manufacturers.

2.1 OPC UA Based RL-OT Integration

Addressing the principles (iii) and (iv) introduced in Sect. 1, [8] proposes an OPC UA based architecture for RL in the context of industrial control systems. OPC UA allows communication between various industrial devices, including both real and simulated devices. The proposed architecture uses OPC UA nodes to extend the standard RL setting. The mapping of the RL action and state space with the OPC UA address space is performed by the RL mapper. The agent's action is turned into an OPC UA call using a function that sets the corresponding actuators using the client-server model. The environment is notified of each sensor change using the PubSub mechanism, mapping OPC UA sensor nodes to RL states. After each sensor change, a reward evaluation is triggered and a state space transition occurs. The paper also discusses how custom object types can be

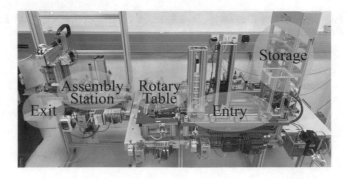

Fig. 1 Model factory placed in the smart factory lab

---

[1] https://its.fh-salzburg.ac.at/forschung/smart-factory-lab/.

created for nodes accessible to the RL agent to automate the mapping between the RL action and state space with the OPC UA address space. This architecture allows for a seamless integration of different out-of-the-box implementations of RL agents into OT systems.

2.2 Integration of Different RL Agents

Kozlica et al. present a simulation environment for a production line in which an agent controlled by RL algorithms transports and assembles goods [4]. The goal is to test the performance of different RL algorithms and their ability to solve the given task. Two different reward functions are defined and compared. The first reward function only focuses on correctly assembling and sorting the products, with no penalty for a simple transition. The second reward function also considers the number of transitions needed for task completion. Negative rewards are assigned to collisions, incorrectly sorted products, and invalid transitions. A positive reward is assigned for completing the task. Moreover, two different RL algorithms are compared: Deep Q-Learning (DQN) and Proximal Policy Optimization (PPO). The results show that both agents can learn to solve the production line task, with the PPO agent generally outperforming the DQN agent in terms of task completion and reward. The authors conclude that the presented simulation environment is suitable for testing and comparing different RL algorithms for the production line task.

3 Conclusion

Our proposed test bed aims to demonstrate how RL can be used to address the demands posed by Industry 4.0, particularly in relation to the four design principles decentralized decisions, technical assistance, interconnection, and information transparency. The test bed consists of a modular production plant and is used for different research based scenarios. In this paper, the authors have shown how to fulfill the Industry 4.0 design principles by incorporating an OPC UA information model in the general RL setting. Additionally, it was shown, that different already available RL agent implementations can be used for solving the defined sorting task.

References

1. Harb, J., Riedmann, S., Wegenkittl, S.: Strategies for developing a supervisory controller with deep reinforcement learning in a production context. In: 2022 IEEE Conference on Control Technology and Applications (CCTA), pp. 869–874 (2022). https://doi.org/10.1109/CCTA49430.2022.9966086
2. Hermann, M., Pentek, T., Otto, B.: Design principles for industrie 4.0 scenarios. In: 2016 49th Hawaii International Conference on System Sciences (HICSS), pp. 3928–3937 (2016). https://doi.org/10.1109/HICSS.2016.488
3. Kober, J., Bagnell, J.A., Peters, J.: Reinforcement learning in robotics: A survey. Int. J. Robot. Res. **32**(11), 1238–1274 (2013)
4. Kozlica, R., Wegenkittl, S., Hirländer, S.: Deep q-learning versus proximal policy optimization: Performance comparison in a material sorting task, submitted to 32nd International Symposium on Industrial Electronics (ISIE)
5. Mahnke, W., Leitner, S.H., Damm, M.: OPC Unified Architecture. Springer Science & Business Media (2009)
6. Nian, R., Liu, J., Huang, B.: A review on reinforcement learning: Introduction and applications in industrial process control. Comput. Chem. Eng. **139**, 106886 (2020)
7. Riedmann, S., Harb, J., Hoher, S.: Timed coloured petri net simulation model for reinforcement learning in the context of production systems. In: Behrens, B.A., Brosius, A., Drossel, W.G., Hintze, W., Ihlenfeldt, S., Nyhuis, P. (eds.) Production at the Leading Edge of Technology, pp. 457–465. Springer International Publishing, Cham (2022)
8. Schäfer, G., Kozlica, R., Wegenkittl, S., Huber, S.: An architecture for deploying reinforcement learning in industrial environments. In: Moreno-Díaz, R., Pichler, F., Quesada-Arencibia, A. (eds.) Computer Aided Systems Theory-EUROCAST 2022, pp. 569–576. Springer Nature Switzerland, Cham (2022)
9. Sutton, R.S., Barto, A.G.: Reinforcement Learning: An Introduction, 2nd edn. MIT press (2018)

Author Index